DOROTHY Y

THE CRY
OF
A BIRD

ALISON HODGE

First published by William Kimber and Co. Ltd. in 1962.
This edition published by Alison Hodge, Bosulval,
Newmill, Penzance, Cornwall TR20 8XA, in 1989.
© Copyright William Kimber and Co. Limited, 1962.
This edition © Alison Hodge, 1989.

British Library Cataloguing in Publication Data

Yglesias, Dorothy
The cry of a bird. – 4th ed.
1. Cornwall. Mousehole. Bird sanctuaries.
Wild Birds' Hospital and Sanctuary.
Mousehole. Biographies.
I. Title
639.9'782'0924

ISBN 0-906720-18-4

To Audrey

Printed and bound by A. Wheaton & Co. Ltd., Exeter.

PREFACE TO THE NEW EDITION

Since *The Cry of a Bird* was first published in 1962 the Sanctuary has had to face two severe crises. These are fully described by Miss Yglesias in her second book *The Answer to the Cry,* but as this has long been out of print it may be of interest to mention them briefly here.

The first crisis was caused by the wreck of the *Torrey Canyon,* an oil tanker, on the Seven Stones reef not far from the Land's End in March 1967. As a result, a huge oil slick spread black and tarry liquid all around the coast, devastating marine life and causing suffering and death to innumerable sea birds, many of them caught while on migration. Day after day, for weeks, hundreds of sea birds – over 8,000 altogether – were brought in, while the Yglesias sisters with the Warden and staff worked desperately to clean, dry, and feed all those who had a chance of life.

The second crisis was of a different kind. In 1960 Dorothy and 'Pog', feeling that the work of the Hospital was getting too much for them, had handed over the whole property to the RSPCA to take over and maintain, confident that its long-term future would thus be secured. Suddenly, in January 1975, the RSPCA found that it could no longer afford to keep up the Hospital, and gave notice that it must close within a month. Dorothy and Pog, though now in their mid-eighties, at once took up the challenge: they decided to use their savings of £500, and with the loyal support of the staff kept things going until a public appeal could be launched. Quickly a local committee was formed, chaired by Mr 'Bill' Young, JP, a Mousehole man, and soon money came in from all sides, donors ranging from local pensioners to the Aga Khan. Mobil Oil gave generous help and made a film of the Hospital's work. Miss Dorothy became President, and on her death Sir Nevil Macready Bt., CBE, then Chairman of Mobil Oil, took her place, and maintains an active interest. The Hospital became a registered charity in 1975.

Crises such as these are a challenge to courage and initiative, but these qualities are equally needed in the day to day work, often in very trying conditions, of feeding, treating, comforting, and eventually restoring to freedom the birds in the Sanctuary's care – often more than 100 at a time. Over the years there has been steady development. New and better pens have been provided, repairs made to the main building, and improved techniques and equipment used for the oiled birds, many of which are still brought in. A shop provides attractive gifts, information and a profit – much needed, for the Hospital depends on help beyond that given by the subscribers. It has always been its policy that admission should be free, so that all those interested can see the work that is being done. For all its activities the lead is given by Olga Penrose who has served for twenty-six years and shares her skill, experience and enthusiasm with her staff, and keeps in touch with subscribers in all parts of the world.

Dorothy Yglesias' work was recognised by the award of the MBE in the New Year Honours of 1980 – sadly, too late for her to share the honour with her sister, who had died in 1977; and Dorothy was too frail to go to Buckingham Palace. She died a few weeks later, and her ashes were buried by her sister's in the grounds of the Hospital.

'Now, what of the future, when we are no more? Will the Sanctuary still hear the ring of Neil's bell? The sound of many wings, soaring to freedom, resting in contentment or folded in the final peace? Will the loving hearts and willing hands be there to hold the course we have tried to set?'

These were Dorothy's closing words in this book. Today, twenty-seven years later, the answer to these questions can be 'Yes', thanks to the inspiration she has given to all those who in many and various ways, carry on her work for the birds.

January 1989
LAURA C. JEWILL HILL
Chairman of the Council of the
Mousehole Wild Bird Hospital

PREFACE TO THE 1973 EDITION

It is forty-five years now since we started with one wounded bird, and eleven years since this book first appeared, describing how from this first small patient our work grew and expanded into the Mousehole Wild Birds' Hospital and Sanctuary.

A very dark shadow fell in 1967 when the huge oil tanker, the *Torrey Canyon*, foundered off Cornwall and the black death of oil was cast upon the sea. The tragedy was overwhelming – a heartbreaking time as so few of the helpless bird victims could be saved. But one great good came out of it, and that was the instant response of the public. At the first news of the ship striking the rocks and the oil escaping, letters offering help, and with gifts of money, came pouring in.

The RSPCA are in close touch with Newcastle University who are making an intensive study of the rehabilitation of oiled birds. This society, and many other organisations, are helping financially. The work has also been given financial support by most of the main oil companies.

We have been surprised and encouraged beyond words by the wonderful letters and responses *The Cry of a Bird* brought, expressing belief that our efforts over the years had been worthwhile. They came from Australia, New Zealand, India, Hong Kong, Africa, America and Canada, and from most countries in Europe and all parts of the British Isles. The writers seemed to appreciate above all that we used the name "Sanctuary" in the real sense of the word – a place of refuge for birds in dire need with restoration to freedom the ultimate aim. The decision to end life was only taken when hopeless suffering demanded it – those birds unable to return to the wild we tried to compensate, making every effort to understand their individual needs. Such birds have themselves shown us that life still holds something for them. For example, Hedger the herring gull, now in her thirtieth year, is still here, peaceful and content. And Neverest, the jackdaw, who flew freely for much of his life, is now aged twenty, and living happily with Pog in her Studio. (Both their stories can be found in Chapter IX.)

To the RSPCA who have generously taken over the Hospital and Sanctuary we entrust these basic principles on which our work was built. Our grateful thanks go to the present staff for all the hard work and sympathetic care they give to this end.

Our deep gratitude goes to our publishers who are now ensuring that the cries of the birds shall once more be heard in the land.

Mousehole, January 1973   DOROTHY AND PHYLLIS YGLESIAS

AUTHOR'S PREFACE TO THE FIRST EDITION

This book has been written not only to show how, from a very small beginning, the work of The Wild Birds' Hospital and Sanctuary has grown and established itself, but also with the aim of enlarging human understanding of bird life, and especially bird character.

The distinctive psychological and emotional characteristics of wild birds are something rather different from their physical habits and behaviour. The latter are capable of investigation by the normal scientific methods of trained ornithologists, observation, statistical records and so on, handled by experts with whom my sister and I have never tried to compete.

In our belief a somewhat different approach and method are needed for the deeper understanding of what a bird thinks and feels, which we believe to be possible, though relatively unexplored. We do not claim that inferences drawn by us from our long daily practical experiences of living with birds should necessarily be accepted as having cast-iron scientific validity.

We do suggest, however, that many of the actual occurrences described in the book may well bear the construction we place on them, and that, if so, they point to a fuller and more sensitive mental and emotional side to bird character than has generally been accepted.

I should like to add that, while not a professional writer, nor an ornithologist, I have tried to set down with complete truth all we have seen and to state it as clearly and accurately as possible, hoping such testimony may be of some value to a further understanding of bird life.

CONTENTS

'The cry, as of a falling bird,
will come like the echo of truth
to the climber of heights.'

Lines written by Pog while at school.

CHAPTER I

THE INVOLUNTARY HOSPITAL

IT all began thirty-one years ago with a drainpipe and a jackdaw. The bird had a shattered wing; the drainpipe was her only refuge until brought to us. My sister, Phyllis (whom we nick-named Pog), was an artist, and I a flower-grower for the market, both very much occupied in our different ways. All that followed was never planned or premeditated by us. Little did we think that our drainpipe Jacko was to become the first patient in what was later known as The Wild Birds' Hospital and Sanctuary at Mousehole.

It was many years before that, in 1912, that we first came to this fishing village in Cornwall for our summer holidays. At that time I had just left school, Pog was studying as an art student in London, and Mary, our youngest sister, was still a schoolgirl.

Having come down by train from London, we were met at Penzance station by a horse-drawn wagonette, the driver of which had only one arm. This added greatly to the exciting final stage of our long journey.

Leaving Penzance behind, the wagonette jogged westwards for the three miles to Mousehole. Through Newlyn, a rather sombre-toned fishing village with granite cottages rising in tiers up the steep hills. Then past the stone quarry where we were held up by the blowing of a warning horn. The charges of dynamite went off, followed by the thunder of blasted rock. Next came the "All clear" of the horn and once more we set off.

The cliff road now followed close to the shore, and the impression still lingers of the beauty made by forests of wild mustard swaying in the breeze against the background of the blue sea. When we came to the steep hill taking us down into Mousehole, the reins were held between the driver's knees while he applied the brake with his one useful hand. We clung to the sides of the swaying wagonette, our mother petrified, but Pog, Mary and myself were in such a state of happy anticipation that we felt no fear. Suddenly the hill ended in a sharp turn and there was the end of our journey.

The road led round the small harbour over which the seagulls circled and called. Perhaps an augury of what was to come? The village consisted of granite houses and cottages, irregular in size and shape, all different in character yet blending into a harmony of grey and white. They were clustered round the harbour, the beautiful curves of which seemed to enfold them from the sea. Landward, on either side, the village was enclosed by gentle rounded hills. The southern one had a tremendously steep road-way hewn out of its side, leading to farms and the country beyond, and this is where we were later to live.

The harbour, in those days, was full of pilchard boats whose deep brown sails would spread before the wind as they silently passed through the harbour mouth in the twilight of the summer evenings. In later days, when we had made many friends amongst the fishermen and their families, we sometimes went to sea with them in their pilchard drifters. Those nights, the peace and the silence, we shall never forget. No noise from motor-boats then; only the ripple of the wind in the sails. How proud we were of being aboard the *Boy Phil*, the lugger with the highest mast of all, or on the *Mur* "PZ.310", a neat little boat with a dandy rig.

It was on that first evening, as we turned the Post Office corner, that we lost our hearts to Mousehole and its people—the village that was eventually to become our home.

With schooldays over we stayed longer every year, but it was not until 1925 that we actually went to live there, giving up our old home in St. John's Wood. Our father, who was an artist, had died some years before, and our mother now decided to build a new home high up on the steep hillside above Mousehole, on a lovely piece of land she had previously bought. It consisted of little flower-meadows and an old orchard, with Mount's Bay, far below, stretched out before it. We called the house Cherry Orchard as the land was full of wild cherry trees, and Pog had a wooden hut put up in the wildest corner of the land to use as a studio.

It was then that the wild birds first came into our lives. How do things begin? By one conscious act or by a semi-conscious desire to atone in minute degree for the sorrow and cruelty of the past ages of mankind? For us it was never what we "ought" to do but what we "had" to do—just a spontaneous response to the cry for help from a wounded bird, a jackdaw seeking shelter in a drainpipe.

Actually it was our sister Mary who had been responsible for this first patient in 1928. When we finally settled in Cornwall, Mary decided to make her living by running a taxi in Goldsithney, an old village five miles east of Penzance. Her car was a "Tin Lizzie" or "Flying Bedstead" Ford, comical and uncomfortable, but high in the air and giving lovely views of the country. One day she found a wounded jackdaw down a drainpipe in her garden; she rescued it and discovered later it had been shot in the wing and had flopped into the back garden of the Trevelyan Arms, one of the two village pubs. The publican, not wanting to destroy it, had put it over Mary's gate knowing she would do something about it. She picked up Jacko (which is what she called the bird—but we discovered later Jacqueline would have been more appropriate) and took her at once to the vet. Unfortunately the wing was too bad to save, so, as she had a stray cat at home, she decided to bring her over to us at Mousehole.

Pog prepared a dark corner of her hut for Jacko, fixing up low boughs and making it comfortable for her to sleep in. She settled down most contentedly and was soon indulging in ecstatic baths, a sure sign that a bird feels at home. She was, however, very modest about these ablutions, and, as a preliminary, would drape strips of paper and oddments of rags over the barricade which was supposed to keep the bath in some sort of bounds.

About this time Pog was commissioned to carve an almost life-sized crucifix in memory of Canon Rogers, the greatly-loved late Vicar of St. Mary's Church, Penzance. It was to hang in the church at St. Hilary, a lovely little hamlet beyond Goldsithney. As the work grew, space became limited, and Jacko did not help matters because she would play about amongst the chips which flew from Pog's chisels.

So a smaller hut had to be added especially for Jacko, to lead out of Pog's. From this the bird could get into an outdoor wire-netting enclosure where we put boughs of apple, cherry and elder trees to make it seem as natural as possible, as it looked as though she would be with us for life. The whole structure was rather perilously perched on the steep hillside, and when we planted primroses and other wild flowers in the pockets of earth amongst the rocky foundations a friend called it our Hanging Gardens of Babylon.

The Cry of a Bird

Soon after this we were to have a second patient. A man living nearby was walking in the woods one day and found a jackdaw with a badly damaged wing. Knowing about Jacko, he immediately brought the bird to us. We dressed the wound and found the wing was not broken, but appeared bruised and slightly out at the shoulder. The bird was very tired and lay in a fluffy heap on the ground with its bad wing outstretched. We called him Muffin, as it seemed somehow to suit him.

When Muffin had recovered slightly, we introduced him to Jacko; and they at once struck up a friendship and lived happily together through that winter. In the spring they mated and built a nest on a shelf up in a corner of the hut. Pog gave them sticks, thinking anything would do, but soon discovered they must be ones in which the sap is dry but the wood is not rotten. They never used them straight from the hut floor where she dropped them, but each one was carried into the outdoor run, tested, and approved or abandoned according to suitability. Moss that Pog carefully dried, thinking they would like it that way, was carried out, washed in the bath, and spread out in the sun to dry before it was used for building the nest.

We thought the babies-to-be were going to have silk pyjamas because all scraps of materials, including sackcloth, velvet, cotton, flannel and wool were discarded for silk.

Five eggs appeared in May, but in spite of all these preparations they did not hatch out.

Muffin had now been with us for over a year. By July his wing was carrying him perfectly as he flew about in the run, although it still drooped slightly at the shoulder as the result of his original injury. We decided to release him, as, with the mating season over, he and Jacko were more independent of each other. He flew off beautifully, returning daily for food. We could always recognize him because of his drooping wing.

We have often wondered what would have happened if Jacko had not broken her wing. Would there ever have been a Hospital for Wild Birds at Mousehole? Without doubt Muffin, our second bird, came because someone had heard about Jacko. So also came our next birds, two fledgling jackdaws.

A friend of ours had brought her small son, Paul, over to see Jacko. The next day they were on the cliffs near their home, the other side of Mount's Bay, when they heard the rather feeble sound of baby birds calling. There were no adult birds in sight, but

4

following the direction of the cry they saw a nest with two fledgling jackdaws in it. They kept a watch for some time and felt the poor little things could not be left to die; Paul finally settled the problem by saying, "Let's take them over to Jacko."

So they arrived, nest and all, and very weak. We kept them warm and put the nest inside a bigger basket, covering them with a little flannel blanket. We were very pleased when they began almost at once to eat soft food off a paint brush. When they had got hold of life again we decided to let Jacko take over; we being completely ignorant about everything. So we put the basket of babies into the hut, with a pan of soft mash beside it, shut the door, and looked through a hole in it to see what would happen.

Jacko then taught us our first lesson. She perched on the edge of the basket, scornfully flung off our covering, and the babies' heads shot up with gaping, yelling mouths. Jacko solemnly looked down their throats, calmly *removed* some of the food we had given, dropped some of her own saliva down their throats and then ignored them completely. She never fed them as we had hoped. She left us to do that, but regulated the amount we gave, and supplied the juices we could not produce.

So we learnt our lesson—never overfeed a baby bird.

We also saw for the first time Nature's wonderful provision for keeping a nest clean while the young ones are still living in it. Each baby, when passing its droppings, would raise its little behind up to the level of the nest edge (sometimes almost standing on its head to do it!) and then the droppings were expelled over the edge, enclosed in a minute bag. This container is fine as a cobweb, yet perfectly able to hold the contents, and if the parent bird wishes to remove it wholesale it can do so. We ourselves have been able to take one up in our fingers, very delicately, and remove it, without breaking, if the babies have not quite cleared the edge.

Max and Moritz, as we named Jacko's foster-children, grew into beautiful young jackdaws and when released eight weeks later we were taught our second lesson—how completely different in temperament and character two birds from the same nest can be. Both were reared in exactly the same way, yet Max was shy and wild, and did not ever come inside the hut again after release, whereas, when first released Moritz flew off, but soon returned, rushing at us with open beak and flapping wings, his

5

feathers rising with pleasure and his little face expressing intense excitement, and almost confusion at the size of the world into which he was now launched. He clung frantically to our heads and shoulders as if to make quite sure we were still there. He continued to show this confidence and friendliness towards us, coming in and out of the windows and daily returning for bath and breakfast for over a year; he would often join us in the garden for meals, behaving like one of the family.

This first instance of a wild bird's trust was a most wonderful experience. "Wonder" was the right word. We had never dreamt of finding such a beautiful way into another existence.

Muffin, in the meantime, had the bad taste to return constantly to the top of poor Jacko's enclosure flaunting his infidelity, "the other woman", before her eyes. Jacko made a few angry remarks then retired inside. The "affair" could not have been a very serious one because it only lasted until the autumn, when Muffin came home alone. We noticed he was holding up one foot, and when he put it down the leg was out at a slight angle. We opened the little window in Pog's hut, and after a wary look round outside he came in, seemed pleased to be home and then deliberately went to the door leading into Jacko's hut, showing us plainly he wanted to be let inside. Jacko was evidently willing to let bygones be bygones, and greeted him with happy recognition.

Muffin's leg gradually got back to normal, and, though we opened the window often to give him the opportunity of flying off, he never wanted to leave Jacko again. They spent the next two years in great contentment and had six eggs during this time, in the old nest, but again none of them hatched out.

One day in February Jacko would take no food. Muffin sat beside her, concerned and watchful, and we gave her everything we could to tempt her to eat. There seemed no reason for this change in her usually fit condition; but in the morning, only twenty-four hours later, she died. We were very upset, and as her death was such a mystery, we asked our veterinary surgeon to have a look at her to find out what had caused it. He found worms inside her and sent away a specimen for identification. It was a "thorn-headed worm, nearly always fatal". Muffin must have got the same affliction, because he too died soon after of the same trouble, again only off-colour for about twenty-four hours. We missed them both greatly.

We noticed when Jacko died, what we have since seen with other birds, that while she was ailing Muffin looked after her, preening her feathers with great affection, but, once death came, he seemed to accept it absolutely, and took no further notice of her when life had flown. Another thing we discovered with Jacko, and later noticed in other jackdaws, was, that when we were trying to catch her she would never allow us to do so until she had given us a definite hard peck on the hand. It was as if she was giving us "permission". Once given, she would sit quite still, and let herself be picked up and carried without resistance.

Later on we had another baby jackdaw, Peter, with specially endearing ways. He was found by some boys in a courtyard, unable to fly. They brought him straight to us, and insisted that as they got to our door, the bird had said, "Quite right, here." Peter was reared up rather exclusively by Pog, to whom he was greatly attached; he was one of the dapper, healthy-looking young ones who grew without any set-backs. When released, he returned to sleep for a week, after that he always slept out, but returned daily for meals. Pog was sleeping in the garden at that time. One morning, very early, before she was awake, Peter arrived for breakfast. When he got no response to his calls for food he sat on her pillow and she was awakened by a very gentle beak just touching her cheek and trying to lift her eyelids.

One day, during those first years, we were reported for "keeping wild birds in captivity". We were told some well-meaning stranger had made a protest. But when our motives were made clear and understood, approval took the place of condemnation. We did not want others to get false impressions, so for the first time we nailed up a board, clearly to be seen from the road, on which Pog inscribed "Jackdaws' Hospital".

Later we added the word "Sanctuary", using the word in its true meaning—a place of safety, even as the holy places of old gave protection to the helpless and persecuted. Our first aim was always to heal, and return the bird to freedom. But if their injuries were beyond repair, we felt life still held something for them, if contentment and peace of mind could replace fear and hunger. By finding sanctuary here many escaped the death that would inevitably have overtaken them in the wild. Those beyond our help at least died without further harm befalling them.

The Cry of a Bird

The board led to many enquiries and increasing numbers of birds of various kinds being brought to us. To make room for the newcomers big wooden boxes with wire-netting doors had to be suspended from the ceiling of Pog's hut, and shelves and corners were made available for them. One end we partitioned off with wire-netting to make separate quarters for seagulls. Great black-backed gulls, kittiwakes, guillemots, rooks and crows, thrushes, blackbirds, sparrows as well as jackdaws now had to be provided for.

The birds had now taken possession of Pog's studio. The time had also come to fix the Christ she was carving onto a plain cross of black wood and there was not the room to do it. So a new studio had to be built of stone to make a permanent place for her to work in, and when the carving was finished it was taken there to be assembled. When all was completed the day came for its dedication and Pog, much against the grain, went to the lunch given at the Vicarage for the Bishop of Truro and other dignitaries, before this memorial to Canon Rogers was conse-crated. The only hat she possessed was an old black sombrero type, discarded by her friend, the artist Laura Knight, and cher-ished by Pog to wear at funerals (the only time she went to church).

After lunch Pog seized a hat and was going over to the church, when she realized the others were not with her. A commotion was going on, the Bishop could not find his hat! With sudden concern Pog looked at the one in her hand, it was black all right, but hers had no trimming. This one was draped with "bootlaces". In much confusion she put matters right, and the aesthetic Bishop prepared for the solemn service with a humorous look on his face that Canon Rogers would have shared to the full.

When the Christ had gone to St. Hilary it was not long before the wild birds began to make free of Pog's new studio. The first to take up residence there was Mrs. Flittertwit. She was a sparrow about whom Pog wrote in her diary:

> "Discovered to be roosting on a beam. Expects breakfast on get-ting up and supper before bed. Invites all her gentlemen friends in to eat but they are chased out at bedtime. Isn't afraid of starlings. Sleeps in on wet nights. Finds box on beams. She drapes streamers of bright darning wool from it. Suppose it's a nest. Then lusty

8

'cheeps' come from another beam. Nest unadorned and invisible. The box and wool are an inverted form of camouflage."

Mrs. Flittertwit reared her family and they all made free of the studio, coming and going as and when they liked, and taking no notice of Pog—thus, in their own way, once and for all dedicating the studio to the use of all "bird-kind".

CHAPTER II

JACKDAWS SHOW THE WAY

JACKDAWS undoubtedly outnumbered all other patients to begin with. Living in London as we had done, we had never even seen one until we came to Mousehole. We realized then how much they are a part of the Cornish landscape—the "chaws" of the villages who nest in the chimneys, the "daws" of the cliffs where they nest in the caves, and the "jacks" of the old mining shafts.

These birds perhaps accept humans more readily than most wild birds. Maybe this was the reason small boys, on finding half-fledged jackdaws young enough to tame, used to take them home and cut their wings to prevent them flying away. They carried them about on their shoulders, or held them perched on sticks to show off to their friends. Our first sight of these poor little mopey birds distressed us greatly, but afterwards we realized it was not lack of kindness but a desire to have something of their own to love, and to be proud of, that led the boys to do it.

Long before the days of Jacko, Pog actually persuaded one very tough boy to let her take care of his baby jackdaw, while he was to come every day to prepare and give it food, clean its house, and let it exercise its wings in a safe place—thus making the bird as happy as he could, to compensate it for having had its freedom deliberately taken away. This the boy did, and although the poor bird eventually died, a new idea was sown in the child's mind which gradually spread to all the children around.

After the Hospital came into being, every June brought its casualties of baby jackdaws, each bird intensely individual as all birds are. The absolute trust of any young thing, completely unaware of danger, is very moving, and anything more appealing than these little bundles of soft feathers and wondering blue eyes, it is hard to imagine. They made us more fully understand the small boys who had not been able to resist the sight of them.

Some of these babies were found dropping with sleep, or staggering with exhaustion, if they had been lost for some time. Some, having fallen down a chimney, were covered with soot; others suffered from concussion, having struck a rock when falling from a nest on the cliffs. All needed help, food and warmth; and the very young needed a nest to replace the one from which they had fallen.

They accepted us as "mothers" usually at once, though some, of course, were more reserved than others. This trust sometimes led to difficult situations, a curious two-way pull arising, as in the case of Rags, a baby jackdaw, brought in very young and very grubby. Pog reared him in her hut and he became devoted to her. One day she saw an adult jackdaw walking outside on top of the run, with full crop and making "chucking" sounds to Rags, who by this time was flying well and quite ready for release. Pog thought this a heaven-sent opportunity, so she took Rags on her hand and put him outside, near the mother bird. At once the mother let off a terrible warning cry to tell the child of the awful danger from the human. Poor Rags recognised the warning but ran for protection to Pog! By that time the mother became frantic, but bravely stood her ground. Finally, Pog managed to launch the baby without being seen by the mother and at once all was well. Rags went up to the mother with fluttering baby wings and "chaws" of anticipation. The mother gave beautiful maternal "chucks" and fed Rags over and over again. At last they flew off together and we felt sure it must be the real parent bird. Later we had confirmation that it probably was so in an interesting way.

We had seven or eight baby jackdaws inside the run when a mother jackdaw came and strutted about on top of it, her crop full and making "chucking" sounds. All the babies answered her but *we* had to make the choice. We picked out the fattest and strongest and took him to the release window. He ran up to her "chawing" excitedly, she turned her back and continued to "chuck" to the others inside. He rushed back to us, the make-shift mothers, who were better than no one. Three times we chose the wrong baby and then the wise mother bird showed us which it was by feeding it through the wire netting. The babies are not particular about the mothers, but the mothers appear to know their own babies.

By 1930 we had a self-appointed Superintendent of the Hospital in Ben the Jackdaw. As a fledgling that May he had fallen down the chimney into the cottage of a fisherman called Ben Jeffery. He was reared up as one of the family and released when fully grown. He flew freely all day but returned to the cottage to sleep at nights. His intelligence was amazing. He could recognise the fisherman's two boys, Tom and Ashley, and land on their shoulders, picking them out from all the children in the school playground. The family later had to move to a new cottage right in the middle of Mousehole with no garden as the old house had. With Ben's real interest at heart they decided to flit while Ben was out. Dusk fell in the new home and they were thinking of Ben when suddenly there was a cheerful "chaw" outside. He had found them and come unbidden to the housewarming.

Later Ben's wings got damaged and the fisherman's wife brought him to us to care for. In eight months he was quite fit again, but he now so loved his new job of bossing, hindering and helping us that he refused to do more than fly about the garden. He made the hut his home, returning at night to sleep inside.

At one time he shared the hut with a Little Owl, and a tame white dove. The latter belonged to a friend, who asked us to look after her while he was away. He assured us she was as pure as a lily and would never look at any other bird even when he let her fly in the garden. At nights we put her in Ben's hut, but in the day she was in our only available run, next to a great black-backed gull. We watched to see if the dove would be alarmed. Far from it. The first thing she did was to go as near to the seagull as the dividing wire-netting would allow, and spread her wings in elegant display before him!

The Little Owl was very small, and very tired, when brought to us. First we made him a bed of dry grass. Then he swallowed tiny bits of meat which we put into his mouth, just as a baby bird would. We, in our town-bred ignorance, thought he was just a nestling, he was so soft and gentle. The next evening, when we went to give him a final feed, he was standing upright on a perch. As we approached he closed one eye, appearing to give us a knowing wink, but when we offered food he bit our fingers hard, so letting us into the joke that he was no infant, but an adult specimen of "Little Owl". We at once called him Mr. Wu.

The hut was now turned into a night club. Mr. Wu flying around screeching, Ben, the jackdaw, whooping and hurling him-

self about, apparently delighted at this breach of hospital regulations (all good birds should be in bed); while the dove, unused
to this racket, had a bath after dark, hoping perhaps to preserve
the purity of her colour, if not of her morals.

So Ben's life passed, happy and free to do as he liked, mixing
fearlessly with our friends as well as ourselves (photo, page 112).

One summer, when Ben was about two years old, we were
having tea on our Cherry Orchard lawn with friends from
London, a K.C. and his wife. The conversation was serious and
of world affairs. Suddenly, out of the blue sky, Ben came swoop-
ing down, landed at our friend's feet and then perched on his
knee, feathers rising with pleasure. Talking ceased, the grave,
thoughtful look on the K.C.'s face relaxed and he said, "Oh,
the privilege; oh, the privilege," in an awestruck way. The
confidence of a wild thing certainly does open one's mind to
something extremely beautiful.

When Ben was seven years old he had a very bad moult; we
did all we could but his flight and tail feathers refused to grow.
So now his flying days were over and he had to live entirely
with us. In spite of this, life continued to be very exhilarating for
him and his active mind still made new interests—such as shriek-
ing to the gramophone and tormenting Pog when she was trying
to work.

He loved the voice of Gracie Fields. In the old days when
flying freely, a Gracie record would always bring him in at the
studio window. In great fuss and excitement he would walk
round and round the gramophone trying to out-sing her, "Chacka,
chacka, chaw". Gracie would trill and Ben would scream, and
the whole place was in a frenzy. Her "Punch and Judy Show"
was his favourite record. He would turn his back in silence upon
operas, choristers, and other famous singers—they were a wash-
out—Gracie was the one and only love for him.

A little later on three young jacks were brought in within a few
days of each other. Nigger came first; he had no injury, only a
twisted claw and was not old enough to fly. The friendship of
this bird, lasting ten years, is one of our most valued memories.

Next came Rip, short for Rip van Winkle, as sleep was an
obsession with him. He had an injured claw and even when the
vet was setting it Rip dropped off to sleep. Nigger at once
adopted Rip, fussed over him, and although only a young bird
himself would feed him every time he called for food. Baby birds

always begin by roosting firmly on their two feet, and then as they grow older they roost on one, tucking the other up under them. Rip, who never did anything for himself, continued to stand on his two feet long after the usual time. Nigger's watchful eye noticed this and one evening we saw him gently push Rip's leg up till it was in the right position. He did this nightly until Rip at last did it for himself.

The third baby jack was Bill. He was suffering badly from concussion—eyes shut and no grip in his claws. We gave him water and then put him in a nest of hay on a shelf in a dark corner. Nigger inspected our work, went into the run, returned with a clean straw and a paintbrush and pushed it under the semi-conscious bird. Bill recovered slightly and tried to stagger off the nest, but Nigger was firm and gently forced him back. He kept a strict eye on him and would not allow him off the nest until he was completely restored by the enforced rest. In a few days Bill joined Nigger and Rip in the run.

By July all three were fine birds and ready to fly. We let Nigger go first, having realised what a wonderful sense of leadership he had, and how he seemed to know instinctively what was right for the young ones to do. When released he flew round in a big circle and returned. Next we let Bill go with him and finally Rip; all three kept together and returned inside again after a short fly. The following day we again released all three. Nigger once more took the lead; the other two were close behind him and he led them first to the roof of our house, then to the studio roof, then to the extreme boundary of our land and from there back to the Hospital Hut. Thereafter this was always Rip's territory, and Nigger would not let him fly outside it, except to return nightly to sleep in the hut. He became extremely selfish, always spilling the water pot over when he had had enough himself and doing his best to keep Bill out. Bill was a much stronger bird and Nigger allowed him to fly where he liked. By the end of the year they were all three sleeping out in the wild, but daily returning for food—except for really bad nights in winter when they sometimes stayed inside. For nearly seven years Rip and Bill came and went like this, gradually returning less and less and finally no more.

Nigger was faithful to us for the whole of his life. He seemed to think it was his duty to help us with each year's crop of baby jacks. There was one that was weakly which he took special care of, piloting him for daily flights but always bringing him home at night to sleep. After some months the baby began to fail; Nigger came to look at him daily but appeared to know he ought not to fly again, understanding better than we did that his span of life was nearing its end.

When Nigger was four years old an interesting thing happened. He came daily as usual but filled up his crop to bursting point with soft food, flew off, and shortly returned for more. Then we found a possible explanation. One day a stranger told us how she saw a curious sight from her window down in the village. A pair of jackdaws had a nest with young ones down a chimney opposite her window and at frequent intervals a fine jackdaw came with his mouth full of food. The two parent birds got off the chimney and the visitor went down inside it while the parents strutted about on the roof "chucking". Then the strange jackdaw came up and flew off again for more supplies. We could not prove it for certain, as the babies had flown when I went to look, but felt sure it was Nigger. We certainly did have proof that, year after year, he had looked after our jackdaw babies when they were first launched by us into the world.

He was full of affairs in the spring and one June brought a piccaninny of his own to Pog's studio to show her; finally he took the young one inside and parked him on a beam, going off alone to enjoy his freedom from responsibilities, leaving Pog to baby-sit until he returned to take him off again to their roosting place.

Each year he brought his wild baby to the studio and in between he spent a good deal of time on the beams himself, developing an amazing range of voice, practising his "singing" every evening about five o'clock. Like Ben, he loved Gracie Fields; but his favourite record was "My Ohio Home".

A devoted friendship developed between two jackdaws, living amongst the others in the hut. One was a deserted baby brought in one June with draggled feathers and very blue eyes; the children said, "He must be called 'Bright-eyes' because they are like shining stars." The other, an adult jackdaw, came in the following July with an injured wing and only one eye: he, of course, became Cyclops. Unfortunately his wing never recovered enough for him to fly fully again. Although so different in age, he and the baby made friends at once. The day came when Bright-eyes was ready to go, at first for short flights, and then for hours at a time, but never for the night. By 3.30 p.m. each day he came back home to Cyclops; and they would preen each other's feathers and roost side by side. In January of the next year we let Bright-eyes out as usual at eight in the morning, and then at ten o'clock an awful thing happened—we let Cyclops escape. As we went in at the door he fluttered over our heads and was carried by a strong wind down to the village. We felt terrible, knowing he was not fit enough to fend for himself. We searched everywhere but saw no sign of him. At 3.30 Bright-eyes came back as usual and at once missed Cyclops; he called anxiously and looked everywhere, but at last gave up and roosted alone on the perch.

The next morning I let him out at eight and two hours later I heard Pog running and calling, "Come quickly, Bright-eyes has found Cyclops." Sure enough, there they were sitting on the roof of our house. They came to the ground, and we tried to catch Cyclops but failed. Then Bright-eyes returned to the hut and brought out some food for him, encouraging him to fly the remaining fifty yards but Cyclops could not do it, and just fluttered out of our reach. For two hours we watched them, feeling utterly miserable.

We decided to leave the whole thing to Bright-eyes and went back to the hut. In about fifteen minutes he came in at the window very cock-a-hoop and cheerful, but alone. He said "Chaw-chaw-chaw" to us; and we said, "The heartless little beast does not care, after all." We gave up all hope and were just going, when we heard some boys calling our name and saw they were holding a bird. We held out our hands for what we thought was the new patient and then realized it was Cyclops, safe and sound, only a little wet from the harbour where the boys had saved him from drowning—Bright-eyes had been right to be cheerful. We felt sure he must have seen the rescue and come straight back to tell us the good news, only we had been too stupid to understand.

Cyclops lived with us for three-and-a-half years. Bright-eyes stayed around, always sleeping out, for six years: after that we did not see him again.

CHAPTER III

TAKING SHAPE

DURING the first two or three years we had perhaps only ten or twenty birds brought to us. The 1930's brought increasing numbers, and we seldom had fewer than fifty or sixty birds to look after, including some still in our care from previous years.

Numbers never lessened, and when we had over a hundred, the problem of providing for them became increasingly difficult. We had no money of our own, except what we earned; Pog, by her wood-carving and I by growing flowers and foliage in our Cherry Orchard garden for the market. To portion out our earnings we had a system of tin boxes. One for our own needs (not very many), one for the birds (growing bigger all the time) and one as a "fling box" into which went the odd half-crowns.

Pog had many commissions; and if she was working on something that had to be finished by a certain date, it meant keeping very late hours, as the birds had to be looked after during the day. Fortunately she was a bit of a night-bird herself and found concentration easier when the rest of the world was asleep.

I worked the other way round, getting up early, often in the dark, to pack and dispatch my foliage in the autumn and winter, and my flowers in the spring. I picked them at odd moments between my work with the birds and bunched them in the evening when the other jobs were finished.

We began our work with the birds at 7 a.m. in the summer and 8 a.m. in the winter and never allowed time to worry us, but went quietly on, encouraging our friends to come and see us at mealtimes—which was the only time when we were able to sit still for a bit. The trouble was we never could say when mealtime would be. It was a rule with us to finish our morning round with the birds completely before stopping for the mid-day meal. Sometimes this would be at four o'clock and our friends were confused as to which meal was in progress.

The great problem was the more birds that came the less time we had to earn the money, but we soon learnt that difficulties anticipated became twice as big. So we waited till they arose and then coped immediately as best we could, and kept calm minds and steady nerves, essential to this work.

Although Mother did not quite "approve" of our giving up so much time to the birds, she was tolerant, and let us annex more and more of the Cherry Orchard land where we set to work to improve conditions for them.

We utilised packing-cases and anything that came to hand to make new houses, as the hut was beginning to overflow with our patients. Money given occasionally by friends was spent on wire-netting and timber. This we used to make big enclosures for the seagulls, high enough for them to test their wings; while Pog constructed cement and rock pools to suit each different type of seabird (photo, pages 122–123).

We also got hold of a water-barrel on wheels to save us carrying water in pails up to Pog's hut. The only drawback was it had to be filled with a hosepipe through the kitchen window from the tap inside, and an awful slop of water resulted. This barrel inspired Pog to make a special bath for guillemots, a really deep one, in which they could dive and swim underwater.

All her bright ideas for the birds were absolutely perfect for *them* but entailed no consideration for humans whatsoever. This bath she decided to make in the middle of a path, being the only place where the ground was soft enough to dig down deeply without coming on rock. She did condescend to make a wooden cover on which pedestrians could walk with great care; but when the bath was occupied by guillemots everyone was held up. We called this "The Coronation Bath" because she was finishing it on the day King George VI was crowned. She inserted gay bits of china in the cement bottom as a coronation mosaic. The birds loved it, and even with all the improvements that followed later I don't think anything has ever come up to this bath.

Our chief enemy was the easterly wind to which our cliff, snugly sheltered from the still fiercer sou'west, is particularly exposed.

Perhaps our worst weather ordeal was in February 1936, when a terrible south-easterly gale unleashed its full force on this bit of the coast, and blew continuously for nearly five days. Perched on the hill, we caught the full force. All day we had anxiously watched the weather hoping the wind would drop, but as evening approached it increased. There were no birds in the stormy sky, all had flown inland for shelter. We went up to look at our gulls (ten herring gulls and one great black-backed gull), and found them huddled in a group; they seemed thoroughly scared. The runs were swaying and bending under the storm; our amateur efforts were not proof against nature at her worst. We decided to bring the birds down to the safety of our toolshed. They kept very calm, and even John, the huge black-backed gull, who hated being handled, lay quietly in Pog's arms as she carried him down the steep steps to the shed where he settled down at once on the dry straw we had put ready. Each bird had to be brought down separately as one of us had to steady the other who was doing the carrying. The wind swept in such gusts of fury that we could not stand against it alone.

With the outdoor patients in safety, Pog then went to the hut in which were housed eight jackdaws, five guillemots, a rook, a shag and a razorbill. She decided to sleep on the floor so as to be more able to act quickly if the roof should lift; which it seemed likely to do at any moment, as the hut stood on the highest bit of our land.

The door was nearly blown off its hinges as she entered, but the birds were quiet inside. Only Thimble, the guillemot, got up and joined Pog on her improvised mattress, and expected to be fed from a bowl of fish, at intervals, throughout the night. The gale roared, everything creaked and groaned. Then at two in the morning there was one more sound added to the din; an ominous "flap" which Pog instantly thought was the felt ripping, prior to the roof giving way. Getting up from her distinctly damp bed (Thimble would try to bath in the fish-bowl) she explored where the sound came from, and found it was Nigger, the jackdaw, in a panic and flapping his wings wildly at the sight of a quite young mouse sitting on the bough beside him. Up to now he had ignored the storm and been peacefully asleep.

The next day came torrents of rain which penetrated even through our well-made windows at Cherry Orchard, and Mother went about with a mop and pail drying up the floor and turning back the carpets. Many people living nearer to the sea had to take carpets right up and empty their rooms of furniture, so flooded were they.

The Cry of a Bird

The common question during those days, when we met people in the village, was, "Have you any riffles?"—a riffle, in Cornwall, meaning a blown-off slate.

Many birds were brought in afterwards as a result of the storm. Amongst them a thrush, who was so battered he did not survive, also three guillemots terribly exhausted, as well as badly oiled. Two of these were later released but one was beyond our help, so was a shag that was brought. We called the shag The Abyssinian—he looked so strangely wild after his struggle with the tempest of wind and sea. We did all we could, but the strength had been beaten out of him and he lost the battle for life.

Raging gales, like this one, brought to mind those early days in Mousehole when it was a point of honour to leap out of bed whenever the sound of the lifeboat rocket was heard, and to make our way by hook or crook, by foot or bike, to the scene of the wreck.

On one such night the S.S. *Ansgir* went ashore in Mount's Bay, about half a mile south of Mousehole. She came in broadside on, grinding against the same rocks where in calm summer weather we used later to release our sea birds.

It was in the early hours and pitch black. Directly we heard the rocket we flung on our clothes, Pog stuffing cigarettes and matches up the front of her fisherman's jersey to keep them dry from rain and sea. This was always part of her wreck ritual. As we dressed we heard the sound of horses' hooves going down the hill so knew the ship must be near shore, and that the life-saving apparatus was being called out. The farmer at the top of our hill, in those days, lent his strong farm horses to pull the great wagon which carried the rocket apparatus to the scene of the wreck. Then we heard men's footsteps going up the hill and shouts of "On the Cracker Rocks", so off we went.

The force of the gale was so tremendous it was almost impossible to be heard against it. Pog and I hung on to each other's belts and struggled first along the Coastguard's track and then down the cliff; there were no paths to help us on this wild bit of the coast. Suddenly we saw the ship which was being swept mercilessly by the waves and was surrounded by boiling surf. It was lit up by flares and was so close in on the rocks we were able to see the crew—Arabs and Lascars kneeling on the deck and crying to Allah. Then a dark figure, very breathless, stumbled at our feet and shouted to us (just two dark shadows to him), "Tell them to send the breeches 'bye'." We did not know, at that time, what the words meant, but faithfully transmitted them to the coastguards higher up the cliff.

At once "the apparatus" got busy. The rocket and line fired over the ship, the line of the breeches buoy made fast, and the first man was brought ashore in the basket.

By this time we had scrambled back again down the overgrown gorse and bracken-covered cliff. Standing in a group were six men. Four Arabs or Lascars, one Japanese and one Irishman. The former were shaking with fear and cold, the latter asked us to show them how to get to the top. Pog then brought out in triumph the cigarettes and matches and at once fear turned to eagerness as the men "lighted up" under the shelter of our mackintoshes.

We struggled on, more cheerful now. Having reached our cottage we made them all come in and gave them hot drinks while beds were being found for them in the village.

On a word from the Irish mate those poor shipwrecked men all removed the cushions from our chairs before they rested their weary, soaking wet bodies on them. Most lovely manners in spite of their narrow escape from death.

Then there was a thump on the door. One of our Mousehole fishermen was standing outside, a self-appointed sentinel, till accommodation could be found for the men. He said, "It is not fitty for you maidens to be there with those rough men in the middle of the night!"

Next day the Japanese member of the crew came up with a great basket of red apples. "To thank you," he said with a sweet but inscrutable smile. We asked him in. Mother listened to his talk, in broken English, of his home far away. He said how anxious he was to improve his English, and asked if she would sometimes write to him. This she did, getting simple letters back for many years.

*　　*　　*　　*　　*

But it was not always storm and struggle. Difficulties evaporated under sunny skies. One thing that made these days easier was the cheaper price of fish which was delivered daily by an old fish hawker. It was said, as he went along, he would cry out: "Fresh fish, fresh fish", and under his breath: "Was once, was once". The gulls were not particular but the diving birds were, and many a time we had to dash off to Penzance to get really fresh fish for them. In those days we used our bicycles "Trundle-up" and "Slow-go-round"—they were not very elegant but they got us there.

When this old hawker gave up we did our best to organize a free supply from the Newlyn fishmarket. The fishermen who landed their catches of pilchards there, were sympathetic and more than willing to give us some, if we provided pails into which they could throw them. The market superintendent was also very co-operative but said we must arrange for the collection. The carrier was equally willing, but could not leave his lorry so would have to collect the pails from a given spot near to his stopping place. After exhaustive enquiries we found a simple soul who agreed, for a small sum, to be the go-between, and carry the full pails from the quay to the carrier's lorry.

For a few weeks we had glorious fresh fish fit for an epicure. Then—no fish. Weather too bad—boats not going to sea—or so little caught, none to spare for the birds. We began to appreciate how precarious a fisherman's living is.

We got emergency rations from Penzance for a few days then got our organization going again. Beautiful supplies and everything serene for a week or so. Then the most appalling delivery came—two pails of guts, liver, soft roes, and heaven knows what insides, of large fish. The birds refused to eat any of it. The smell was revolting. We had to sweep it all up from where the birds had dragged it about the runs and then spend an hour burying it in the garden. Good manure, but not the kind of "ill wind" we enjoy. That ended our efforts to get free fish.

Since then we have been supplied by a fishmonger in Penzance who has it sent out daily by bus. He serves us very well and reasonably, either his son or he himself bringing over our Bank Holiday supplies, and keeping the fish on ice in his refrigerator especially for us. It solved our nightmare of stinking fish over long weekends, and we have never failed to appreciate his thoughtfulness.

We tried to give natural things as far as possible and were very careful to give plenty of clean fresh baths and water to drink. When Pog was looking after the seagulls they never went short of this even in the early days when it meant carrying pails of water by hand. Her reward was in seeing the birds' sheer delight at fresh water, and when we got to the stage of taps and hosepipes in the runs, she would let the baths overflow, and the taps run freely, so that the birds could have the actual movement of the running water which they so love.

Gradually we got a little more efficient over the birds' house-keeping but it was rather distracting having to cater for anything from a gannet to a wren without any warning of its arrival, or, to begin with, any knowledge of its natural food. However we improved with time. But always, as from the very beginning, it was the birds themselves that showed us the way.

Chapter IV

FROM ALL THE AGES OF MAN

IT was the children of Mousehole who helped us to build up this Hospital and Sanctuary for Wild Birds. The thought that they were saving lives soon began to stir their imagination. Now when a bird was seen in trouble it was a matter of urgency to rescue it, and bring it to us. As the years went by the idea got deeply rooted, and when this first generation of children grew up, and married, their children in turn carried on.

Ben, our jackdaw superintendent, of course, encouraged all boys, as he adored the noise they made and answered back with excruciating sounds. The boys would whisper naughty remarks to Ben and he would yell, "Quite right, y'are" or sounds to that effect. They brought him "toys" at Christmas, and on one occasion a tiny tin motor car. Ben proceeded to pull off a wheel and wash it in his drinking water, much to the excitement of the boys. He had no fear of them but never forgot that in his early days, in Ben Jeffery's cottage, one of the boys, Ashley, had, by mistake of course, trodden on his foot. One day, when Ashley was in the hut and Ben was hopping about on the floor, he made a direct attack on Ashley's ankle and drove him into one of the enclosures the other end of the hut. This, of course, convulsed the other children.

We have never given any reward or money to the children when they have rescued a bird; I don't think it would ever have crossed their minds, and once, when a cynical grown-up accused some boys of doing it for the sixpence they hoped to get, the boys were furious and so were we.

The children have always had faith in us and what we were trying to do. Once a small five-year-old was found by his mother wrapping a little dead bird in cotton wool; when she said she would bury it for him, he hugged it to him and said, "No! I'm taking it to Miss Gleeshus—she will make it well." "Gleeshus" is the nearest the children can get to our unusual name.

24

From All the Ages of Man

It is sometimes difficult to make the children who rescue birds understand that they cannot have them back to keep as pets when cured; but that they all must return to their own free life. For example Roderick, a boy eight or nine years old at the time, brought us an oiled guillemot requesting its return when cleaned. We explained the bird did not "belong" to him or to us, but to itself. Roderick retired to a rocking-chair in the corner of the studio and, while we were talking to the grown-ups, we heard him muttering to himself, "I *want* the bird, I *want* the bird—it's better for the bird to stay here—it's better for the bird to stay here." Finally he made the big decision and renounced his "rights".

Another renunciation was made by a boy who wrote us a most distressing letter from a city in the North. It was badly written and illiterate, and as there was no mention of home or parents, we sensed some unhappy background. He told us the one thing he loved was a baby jackdaw which he had saved from death, made a little house for, and tended with the greatest care. The bird had returned his love and we could so well understand the bond between them. Then one terrible day he found his bird dead, killed by some boys in the school. He had heard about our Wild Birds' Hospital and sent this heartbreaking letter asking us to let him have another jackdaw. We told him as simply as possible why this could not be done. He understood our reasons, and wrote back asking, "Please may I come at once and learn to be a vet in your Hospital?" We wished we could say "Yes" but were only able to suggest his trying to help at some animal refuge near his home until he was a little older when he could write again; but we heard no more.

Another boy, a visitor from Kent, had an inspiring determination that the young herring gull he had rescued should live. All the symptoms were to the contrary. The bird was almost senseless, unable to stand or eat, and with a terrible wound on his head. We explained the chances were small but the boy challenged us by declaring, "The bird must be called Dauntless." We nursed him with the utmost care, dressing his wound and giving nourishing but small quantities of food at frequent intervals. To our amazement he recovered and three weeks later was ready to be put in the big run with about a dozen adult seagulls. These adopted him at once, allowing him "first bath" and always showing him special consideration. He was rather a "backward child" so we kept him two years. He was then quite recovered and we released him with another gull of his own age. For a long time he returned daily for food, feeding from our hands when really hungry. Then, a few years later, we were delighted when he brought his mate as well and for twelve years they continued to call.

One April, twin boys, seven years old, came holding an injured jackdaw very firmly in their hands. They drew back as we went to take it and one said very sternly, "You do grow new wings here, don't you?"

"We do our very best," we replied, and then were allowed to have the bird. Our "best" failed to save the wing but Twinlet as we called him lived with another permanent inmate, very contentedly, for several years.

Another small boy from Newlyn came one day with two baby jacks. They were not more than a day or so old, their eyes not open, and with not much desire to live. The boy had been helping his mother by sweeping a bedroom chimney. Instead of soot he brought down a mass of sticks with two tiny birds in the middle. Terribly upset at what he had done, he got a box, filled it with cotton wool, wrapped the babies in his best woollen socks, got the first bus to Mousehole and came to us. We shall never forget his face of concern as he watched us trying to make them take notice. We felt desperate, fearing they would die before his eyes. Then, suddenly, two heads shot up and two enormous mouths opened with piercing cries of hunger. We fed them carefully and the boy's face was transfigured with joy. We called them Pepper and Salt. Pepper grew into a wonderful bird, and was released eight weeks later. Salt, though treated in exactly the same way, developed feather trouble and we could not let him go for several years. Eventually his feathers grew; but some always remained white and twisted. Though living freely in the wild, Pepper continued for years to fly in through our open window in one great swoop, right through the sitting-room into the kitchen beyond, and land on my head or shoulder. He never perched on us out-of-doors but only in the hidden security of our room.

The most cruel act we heard of in connection with birds brought to us was that of a farmer who shot a jackdaw and then deliberately hung it up by one leg as a scarecrow *while still alive*. A boy, who has rescued many birds, saw this happening. He waited until the man had gone, then cut down the bird and brought it straight to us. It was bleeding, suffering from shock and the leg was out of joint. In a day or two it began to pick up and became one of our most contented inmates, feeding from our hands and losing all fear. Its feathers had been perfect but after its first moult they came through twisted and some of them white. We wondered if this could have been caused by what it had been through. It was never able to fly again but lived most happily with us for seven years; and in the end just died suddenly in its sleep.

Spontaneous acts of real courage are sometimes performed by children to save a bird, such as that of quite a little girl at Lostwithiel. She was near a burning rubbish dump when she noticed a very young seagull walking, frightened and bewildered, on the smouldering heap. She did not hesitate but rushed to the rescue. Her shoes got scorched; but on she went until she reached the bird whose feet were blistered and feathers burnt. She carried it home and at once it was sent to us. Fortunately, a day or two before, a deserted baby gull had come to us and was now very much at home on the nest of straw we had made for it and already fed confidently from our hands. This helped to overcome Lucifer's (as we called the burned gull) bad experience and it was a pretty sight to see them lying side by side on their nest. They made good progress and were released together as perfect birds twelve months later.

The Mousehole children often wanted to help us during their holidays. We could not let them do anything directly for the birds for fear they might frighten them; but we were grateful to the boys when they enthusiastically swept down the steps, and tidied up outside; or fetched seaweed and cuttlefish from the rocks.

One winter three little girls turned up announcing that they had come "to do some cleaning". They set to work, scoured the paint, cleaned the windows, and helped with the drying up. Their housewifely bustle was almost atomic in its energy, and we felt half an hour of it daily was perhaps enough for all concerned.

One day they arrived late, rather breathless, and carrying between them a very big washing basket full of every imaginable kind of little dish and basin, plate and saucer. With extreme good manners, they gave us to understand that they had noticed, while drying up, that the birds' dishes and pans were old and cracked, therefore they had decided to do something about it. Apparently they had set off that morning armed with the washing basket, and visited all the likely-looking houses in Mousehole. They had informed each lady of the house that crockery was wanted at the Birds' Hospital, and would she please provide some?

27

We asked, rather nervously, if we had been implicated in this, and with one voice they said: "Oh, no, when people asked if you had sent us, we said it was our own idea, that the birds must have new dishes!"

The response was wonderful—the children knew just what they wanted, and they had refused firmly if size and shape did not meet with their requirements.

*   *   *   *   *

We found from the start that the grown-ups, as well as the children, were glad to have some place where their kind impulses could, so to speak, "come to roost". All sorts and conditions of people went to endless trouble to bring us casualties they had found. Some, such as policemen, dustmen, coalmen, conductors and others, have come upon these birds in the course of their work.

One August, three young men, patients at Hayle Hospital, near St. Ives, were convalescing and during one of their walks had found a jackdaw with a damaged wing which they had named Aloysius. They brought him over to us; and a few days later they wrote, enclosing eleven shillings collected in their ward, to help with his upkeep. The letter went on: "There are not enough lovely things in this world that we should wish any of them destroyed. Good luck to you and your efforts, we hope that Aloysius will be restored quickly to health and the freedom of the skies." A month later we were able to write the good news to them that just this had happened.

Once, very early in the morning, an engine driver of the Great Western Railway came to us. He had, on his night journey, unavoidably hit and injured with his engine a beautiful white Barn Owl. He was so distressed by the accident that, tired as he was, on reaching the terminus at Penzance he came straight over to us with it. We much appreciated the way he had put all thought of his own weariness out of his mind, his only concern being how best to help the bird. To our great regret it was one of the hopeless cases and had to be destroyed. Even so, the engine driver felt that it was better than having left it by the wayside.

Another time a young man came, holding a guillemot which he told us he had found badly oiled. He had cleansed the feathers but they remained waterlogged, and the bird was not well enough to release. He, like the twins, seemed reluctant to hand it over.

As he did so he said: "If it cannot be returned to the sea you won't destroy it, will you?"

When we told him, "There are no destructions here except where it would be cruel to prolong life", his whole face relaxed in a smile. This man had been out of work for three months. He had a wife and child to support and had only got employment a fortnight before; and yet when he said good-bye he gave us a pound "to help out".

Another gift inspired by real feeling was that of our coalman who quite often returned our tip saying, "Please put it in the Bird Box."

An appeal was once made to us by an ex-serviceman who had been badly disabled in the last war. He told us how he and his wife had got a very great deal of happiness by befriending a "wounded and bedraggled seagull". The bird was quite unable to fly so they made a special landing stage for him on the pond in their garden and tended him with the greatest care. Then, owing to the bad state of the husband's health, they were obliged to leave the place where they had been living and the problem of what to do with Charlie, their injured common gull, arose. They were both determined that he must still be cared for, though circumstances made it impossible to carry on themselves. Their letters told how worried they had been until they heard of our sanctuary, and knew he could come here.

Although Charlie had to leave the friends without whose loving care he would have died, he soon settled down with us; and having companions of his own kind was a compensation for losing his old protectors.

He lived happily here for seven years and each Christmas a gift came for Charlie and his friends, and even now, long after the gull's death, the soldier with a fellow sympathy for permanent injury continues to send.

Walking on the high cliffs near Mullion one afternoon, a couple visiting Cornwall saw a young wounded kestrel stranded some way below on the overhanging cliff. It was a dangerous job to try to rescue it but the man did not hesitate, lowering himself slowly and carefully he reached the bird, wrapped it in his wife's cardigan, and finally with great difficulty, regained the top. We called the bird Excelsior (Sior for short); we thought the effort was worthy of the name. His rescuers said if we could not save the wing they would like to make a special house and run for him in their Surrey garden, and keep him for life. It gave us real pleasure to meet people who were genuinely prepared to go all out to make up to the bird for his bad start in life, without any thought of the work it would entail for themselves. So when, after everything possible had been done, we failed to save the wing, we felt quite happy to send Sior as arranged.

They took such trouble to get conditions quite right for him, and were so understanding of his needs, that life again became worthwhile for him. Every Christmas a card still comes to us from them and Sior.

One summer day a hoard of young boys came up our steps followed by a man in the habit of a monk, who was holding a seagull in his arms which appeared to have a broken wing. After telling him of our work, in which he was interested, he turned to go. We called to the boys, thinking the monk was in charge of them; but with some shyness he explained that the boys were in charge of *him*! They had commandeered his help in rescuing the seagull caught in a cleft in the rocks and insisting on his bringing it to "The Hospital". The bird's wing, fortunately, was only badly strained, not broken, and it eventually flew off perfectly fit. We called it The Benedictine, hoping we had guessed right.

Soon after this we had a white duck brought to us all the way from Slough, about three hundred miles away. We have had many ducks, but this newcomer, Dolly, of unknown pedigree, was the only one that remained as a permanent inmate. Poultry keepers assured us she was of no known domestic variety so we presumed she was of wild origin. She had lived for two years as a public character on a pond in her home town. Then one winter the pond had frozen over; some boys flung a stone and one of Dolly's wings had been hopelessly smashed.

The people who rescued her, Mr. and Mrs. Holloway, had done their utmost to make her happy, even building a cement bath in their garden, into which she refused to go. Her self-chosen, exclusive diet consisted of worms and digestive biscuits; but when the worm supply neared exhaustion and Dolly's quacking complaints became incessant the Holloways enquired about our sanctuary. Much as they hated the thought of parting with her they felt it might be better for Dolly to come here.

She duly arrived, personally accompanied by Mrs. Holloway. The latter was someone after our own hearts; her only concern

was that Dolly, who had suffered so much, should now be happy.
To this end we dug frantically for worms but Dolly scorned them;
they evidently were not the size she was accustomed to, she would
only look at enormous ones. She would not go in the bath, nor
did she like the house we had prepared for her; so we decided to
put her with the other birds and see what that would do.

We chose the run occupied by Deb and Nan, two oyster
catchers, and Avory, a nerve-case seagull. The two former had
come in a short time before, both with permanently injured wings.
The seagull, a first-year bird, had been suddenly attacked by a
"tiger" cat; the man who saw it happen had quickly driven off
the enemy, but the damage had been done—not with an obvious
wound but to the bird's nervous system. The poor herring gull
was in a state of collapse, could not stand, had no balance and
continually threw his head backwards over his shoulder. When
he was brought to us we hesitated. Was he one whom we ought
not to try to save? He was very young so we thought we would
try for twenty-four hours at least. We put him in a quiet, rather
dark place, and gave him raw egg and special tablets. Next day
we saw a marked improvement and persevered until he could
stand up, keep steady and feed himself; then we put him with
Deb and Nan, both gentle birds, but it was Dolly the duck who
ear-lly completed his cure. She gave the other three birds an auto
cratic look on going into the run, inspecting everything and
swelling with her own importance. But she still would not go
in the bath.

Her new companions were impressed and fell for her at once.
They deliberately went in and out of the bath, time and time
again, till at last she got the idea and plunged in. At night-time
she refused to go into the hut so the two oyster catchers remained
outside in the run, standing as sentinels on either side of her as
she slept on her bed of straw, Nan pointing her long orange beak
to the north, and Deb turning to the south. The next night they
ran in and out of the little door leading to their night-quarters
in the hut, repeating the action many times until once more she
learnt the routine and followed them in.

From now on Dolly exerted an extraordinary influence over
them all and sat like a queen on her nest. She laid ten eggs at
frequent intervals, soon after arrival (photo, pages 82–83).

The seagull's nerves recovered under Dolly's management in
an amazing way, and after a few weeks with her, we transferred

him to the main run, thinking now he would prefer to be with his own kind. But in a day or two he was once more in a state of nervous tremor. Returned to Dolly, he calmed down, and in a very short time was normal again. We now had a psychiatric ward with Dolly as Matron. Even the visitors fell for her, some going so far as to dig worms for her. She did condescend to eat digestive biscuits also, and every Christmas a parcel of them comes from Mr. and Mrs. Holloway, who never forget her.

Two more patients were later put under her care—another oyster catcher and a whimbrel. The latter was sent from Truro with a permanent wing injury. It was very shy until Dolly brought it under her spell; since then it has been very happy to be one of her retinue.

As Dolly got to know us we would let her wander about the paths outside the runs, and she would follow Pog everywhere. But if visitors dared approach she quacked furiously, turning her back on them and insisting on having the door opened into our private garden. There she would remain in dignified seclusion till the coast was clear.

CHAPTER V

PERIL ON THE SEA

B Y now we had learnt how to cope with jackdaws, rooks and seagulls, and with the more ordinary small birds. As we had no real knowledge about birds in general the arrival of a new species meant exhaustive study of bird books, and continual watching of the bird itself to find out what was needed.

How to deal with our first storm petrel was a problem. Though they are one of the smallest of the sea birds, being only about six inches long, their severe-looking beaks and dead-black plumage made us call them "gloomy deans". The name stuck and our exclamation, "Oh, another gloomy dean" led to an astonished look on the faces of those who had found them and brought them to us. Our first one was found creeping about on the road outside our house—he was completely unafraid, only suffering terribly from exhaustion. We were puzzled what to do with him, but he solved the difficulty for us by creeping up inside the warm sleeve of Pog's old jersey. We quickly got a Lyons' Swiss Roll carton, filled it with dry grass, which we cut up small to prevent his tiny feet getting entangled, and then put him on the table in front of it and without hesitation he scuttled inside. Being a night bird he slept all day in his little house except when he was wakened to be fed with a paint-brush dipped in cod-liver oil, raw egg, minced fish liver and guts—this being the nearest we could get to "floating offal", which is what the bird book told us they fed on.

In four or five days he had quite regained his strength, and seemed to be ready to go, so we waited for darkness; then, armed with torches, we took him down to the shore. Pog put him on the flat palm of her hand and held him aloft. He stood quite still, then she felt a strange vibration working through him. This gradually increased, his wings moved faster and faster till they reached a terrific speed. Suddenly, in complete and uncanny silence, he wafted off her hand and out into the night like a great black velvet moth.

33

The Cry of a Bird

Our first guillemot or Rio (the local name for them) was brought to us in 1934. He was a young one washed up in the surf during a bad storm at Sennen Cove. This is a small fishing village that lies tucked under the massive, rock-strewn cliffs about a mile north of Land's End. The little guillemot was swept in on the huge waves, powerless to withstand their strength, yet surviving to be thrown up on the soft sand, exhausted and frightened.

As Pog puts it in her old diary, "His fear is only of the water, which he refuses to drink. Fresh or salt is equally distasteful to him, and the only comment he makes is 'Hic-ic'."

We called him Ajax because he had conquered the storm. As he grew bigger we took him daily down to a pool on the Mousehole rocks, making a special carriage for him out of a wastepaper basket enveloped in a black skirt, drawn up top and bottom with a cord. The result was rather like a black hearse and to it he became devoted.

When quite proficient in diving and swimming we took him (in hearse) back to Sennen Cove where Guy Dollman, the artist, and his wife, joined us to see the grand return to freedom. But Ajax had quite different ideas; after one quick plunge he rushed back to his hearse where he cleaned every feather, surveying us with pitying scorn. We were lunching at the hotel with the Dollmans so Ajax, too, had to be invited. We turned back the black skirt, put the hearse on a chair between us and there he sat quite content through the whole meal, just popping his long neck up occasionally to see how we were all getting on.

So home again we went to Mousehole where he spent the rest of his life with us, happy in his daily routine of swimming in his rock pool on the shore, but absolutely refusing to return to his old enemy, the sea.

Of the hundreds of these lovely birds we have dealt with all these years, three guillemots I shall always remember. They came within a few days of each other, badly oiled. We were very full up at the time so they had to be put in a little room where some of our old books had been piled in the corner awaiting sorting out. In the morning I found the biggest bird had left the others and was perched on top of one of the "Everyman" series so we called him "Everyman" and of course the other two became "I will go with 'ee" and "Ann be my guide". When they were released a few weeks later clean and beautifully strong it amused us to see "Ann be my guide" take the lead, "I will go with 'ee" next and "Everyman" proudly on his feet, last of all (photo, page 151).

After watching them flying and swimming further and further away from the shore, we turned to go home, and then saw another bird threshing through the water at great speed. We went back to the sea edge and waited to see him land, as by this time we realized he was an oiled guillemot. He climbed up on to the rocks a little way off, flapped his wings violently and looked as if about to try to clean off the oil with which his whole breast was covered. We decided we must catch him before he began to do this, knowing the deadly results if he swallowed any in the process. We felt rather brutal as we had to chase him around quite a bit before we cornered him. He was one of the very wild ones, a good sign, as probably the oil had not been on too long. When we caught him he lashed out furiously with beak and wings. We called him Passion because of his rage when first in our hands. This anger was due to the desperate way in which we had approached him on the rocks. Guillemots, as a rule, though highly nervous and sensitive, are gentle and trusting once this initial wildness has quietened down.

Our hands scratched and bleeding, we rushed home with him, gave him some halibut oil forcibly (he was far too annoyed with us to take fish from the hand) and after leaving him alone for about an hour we set to work to clean his feathers. In a day or so his plumage looked perfect, he was feeding naturally and had a large appetite. We encouraged him to swim daily in the Coronation Bath, and this he learnt to do with great skill, considering how wild he had been, and he would dive to the bottom to catch bits of fish underwater when we threw them in.

In four weeks he was strong and fit and we knew it was time for his release, so we took him down to Cracker Rocks where he gazed seawards, stretching out his long sinuous neck, his dull black wings making a striking contrast to his now gleaming white body. His whole shape was streamlined and beautiful. He stood upright on his feet, flapped his wings until great momentum was reached, and then "off", over the surf, and away to the open sea (photo, page 94).

*   *   *   *   *

The razorbill, another diving bird, has much the same coloration as the guillemot, but is slightly shorter in length and has a more stocky and shortnecked build. It has a large round head with small calculating-looking eyes and an enormously strong curved beak with which it can inflict a nasty jab when annoyed. It is perhaps less nervous on the whole than the guillemot—but more turbulent and extremely determined. One we had would make a direct assault on Pog's slacks, or the edge of my apron, and hang on quite regardless of our moving around. This was to ensure "first feed" at mealtimes.

Billie was one of our first razorbills, and came covered with oil. It was very cold weather, so Pog made him a warm corner in her studio. When he recovered he was consumed with curiosity as to what she was doing on her side of the barricade, and each night would push a way through and come and inspect. This proved useful later when he developed a cough for which the vet prescribed an inhalant, but Billie stubbornly refused to co-operate. Pog had an inspiration; she got out an old black cloak that Laura Knight had left behind, draped it like a tent over her head, sat inside with the jar of inhalant, and waited. Sure enough, Billie could not resist finding out what she was doing and poked his way inside where he inhaled happily. Pog nearly suffocated, but that couldn't be helped. This happened each night until he was cured.

Quite a different sort of character was an irresistible baby razorbill found by a Mousehole boy high and dry in a cave crying piteously for its mother. She was nowhere to be seen, so the boy brought him to us. We named him H.M.S. Concord, because once his hungry cries ceased, he became the most placid and peaceful infant. New feathers soon replaced the baby down and he grew apace. We took him down to the shore to give him a swim in a sea-water pool daily for five weeks. He was happy and content, then in the sixth week he suddenly became wild and restless. He had heard the call of the sea, and we knew he was telling us the time had come to say farewell. On a beautiful September day we made our last journey with him to the shore. No hesitation now; he stood a moment on the rocks trying his wings and then away he went, skimming over the calm sea, diving, coming up again and then off for good.

Another razorbill, this time a most determined one, was seen by three boys out fishing. He was badly oiled, and swam for a whole hour round and round their boat. At last the boys threw a basket overboard to see what the bird would do; instantly he jumped inside. They hauled him aboard in this "improvised breeches buoy" (the name we later gave him) and brought him to us. Probably the oil had not been on him very long because it came off fairly easily. He never lost energy or appetite and in two and a half weeks he went off again in perfect condition.

*   *   *   *   *

Then there were the puffins, the little diving birds so full of character and intelligence. Their plumage resembles that of the guillemot and razorbill, but the bird is smaller and has an extraordinary beak, thick and almost parrot-like in shape, portions of it brilliant red and yellow in colour. Their legs are bright orange.

The local name for puffins is "popes", a good one, as it somehow envisages a pontifical dignity combined with a subtle wisdom which for all we know may be common to popes and puffins. One we called Pope John as he came to us at the time of the new Pope's accession.

Some visitors one day found a puffin oiled and exhausted, and took it to the Penzance Police station. The officer-in-charge asked the R.S.P.C.A. Inspector to bring it to us. On arrival he warned us to be careful as he had just been binding up the wounds inflicted by this bird on the police force. The puffin, after one sidelong look out of his strange little eyes, decided all was well now that the hand of the law was no longer upon him. He jumped from the basket onto my lap; allowed us to clean him without protest, and was a perfect patient. His code of behaviour was so good, and his expression so full of wisdom that we called him Confucius. The way a puffin deliberately looks up at you, as if from under invisible eyelids, is something once seen never forgotten.

We kept him in our sitting-room and let him have a daily swim in our own bath; when he had finished he would jump on the edge and stand there solemnly till we lifted him down. Two weeks later he flew up on the back of a chair and gazed out to sea, then next day he went to the closed front door and stood still with his great beak pressed to the crack. The sage had spoken; this evidently was to be the day of reunion with his wild life. We took him down to the rocks, opened the basket and out he jumped, a very different picture from the day he came. After flapping his wings and inflating, he took off beautifully, flying right over the surf and big waves and alighting on the calm water beyond.

One winter three puffins were found wandering about in London, one on Priest's Bridge, Barnes, and the other two on Richmond Bridge. They had probably been blown up river and inland by the bad January gales prevailing at the time. One can imagine the confusion of the puffins at finding themselves amongst giants and juggernauts, with cars rushing by, people all around who did not seem aware of their existence, and worst of all—no sea anywhere. Then someone did see the poor midgets, and rescued them from their plight.

One was taken to the Jermyn Street Headquarters of the R.S.P.C.A. from where he was sent by rail to us. Piccadillo, we called him. And the other two arrived a few days later, from the same source, both as light as thistledown, bewildered and quite exhausted. We put them by our warm airing-cupboard, giving them small doses of halibut oil, and slowly they regained strength. After a week they were strong enough to come into our sitting-room every evening and exercise themselves by running up and down our couch. We called the other two Kontiki and The Small World.

They were all completely different in character. Piccadillo confident and self-possessed; Kontiki, the biggest bird, very calm and rather slow in the uptake. The Small World, though quite adult in plumage, was tiny in size, dapper in appearance and much wilder than the other two. Piccadillo soon got tired of promenading on the couch and decided one night to leap the gap on to the arm of a nearby chair; he leapt back again, then solemnly repeated the performance. Each night he increased his range until finally he flew right up and landed on the shade of the electric lamp, standing on the table where I was writing letters. I saved the lamp and he simultaneously flew to the back of my chair and gave me a peculiar look. Next, Kontiki took off from couch to arm-chair in a ponderous way, obviously under instructions from Piccadillo; and finally The Small World, independent as usual, and scorning armchairs and lampshades, just shot with whirring wings across the room.

Our Collie sheepdog, Dusky, shared the couch with them. Piccadillo, in particular, enjoyed sitting on his warm back or on a cushion beside him (photo, page 84). When the room seemed completely occupied by active puffins we thought it was time to harden them off in one of the huts and let them have an outdoor bath. Up to this time they had had a daily swim in our own bath, filled to the brim. The Small World thought it a poor show, but the other two enjoyed it (photo, page 71).

After a month they were absolutely fit and ready to go. One sunny morning we took them to the rocks, and after flapping and inflating they took off beautifully, The Small World first and Kontiki last. They flew strongly, and the last we saw were three specks swimming and diving as they made for the open sea.

*   *   *   *   *

There is a strange fascination in the gaze of the mysterious-looking shag. It is the bird of the ocean underworld, diving in its shadows, and yet with an extraordinary innocence about it. If the young ones are somehow separated from their parents, they seem quite unaware of the need to hunt for food. They sit on the rocks, getting weaker and weaker, and many we have had brought to us have been too far gone to save. Those that are only just desperately hungry will take fish from the hand, and soon pick up, but, if returned to the sea too soon, back they come to the rocks and wait for a little more public assistance.

One young shag, which had a British Museum ring on his leg when brought to us, was so apologetic in his approach to food that we called him Excuse Me. After release he not only returned to shore three days later, but even went to the length of waddling up the rocks on to the road and waiting outside the Mousehole Post Office, holding up the traffic, till someone took pity on him and brought him back to us. We knew he was Excuse Me returned because of the ring, and also because he behaved in the same way. Sitting firmly in his house he would then stretch his long neck and expectant face round the corner of it, gently taking the fish when offered and retiring modestly to digest it. We kept Excuse Me about seven months, and when he was fully grown there was no difficulty whatever about his return to the wild; and we were able to report his adventures to the Bird-ringing Department of the British Museum.

The Wallaby, another young shag, so called because of the great leaps he made about the run, had an entirely different personality. He snatched food without any sign of manners, and honked for more; but on release, he also returned to the shore, and was sent back to us for further education. After one more month here he went very wild, flying up to a ledge and focussing his eyes on the distant sea. This was our signal. We took him down to the rocks, and this time he seemed to know, absolutely, what to do and went off without hesitation (photo, page 124).

Ulanova, a slightly older shag, was so called because she was an exceptionally beautiful and graceful bird, with all the elegance of a ballerina. She was languid and aloof when brought in one October, but once her appetite got normal (not to say enormous) she revived. She was extremely content with us until the following April, when we released her with another shag, fully restored.

Not long after this Pog was one day having a swim off the lonely Cracker Rocks when an embarrassing situation happened. She heard a shout and saw a neighbour of ours coming over the rock with a frantic look on her face, holding a young shag at arm's length. Pog dashed out of the water seeing something was wrong. She discovered the girl's arms and frock were swarming with bird lice. The little shag was in a bad way, and the lice were leaving his cooling body even as rats leave a sinking ship. Pog took the bird and advised the distraught girl to fling all her clothes off and jump straight into the sea, which she did as there was nobody in sight. Pog did all she could for the bird, and then tried to evacuate the lice from the clothes.

Suddenly the "chug-chug" of an out-board motor was heard, and there, bearing down on them at great speed was a boat, the fishermen in it were coming to look at their lobster pots moored nearby. The girl felt this was the last straw, and in spite of Pog's advice to remain submerged, she climbed mermaid-fashion out of the sea, feeling lousy clothes were better than none.

*   *   *   *   *

Most of our birds in trouble came to us from round about but some came from very much farther afield. For instance one day a great shearwater was sent to us from Southampton. It had arrived on R.M.S. *Caronia* suffering from concussion through having flown against the funnel when in mid-ocean. It was handed over to the R.S.P.C.A. who sent it on to us.

It was still suffering from shock on arrival and was not able to eat for itself, but slept for hours at a time. So we built up its strength with raw egg and halibut oil, till in about three days it was quite a different bird.

We tried it out in the biggest run and it showed us plainly it had recovered, with eyes bright and alert, so we decided to release it. We took it down to a grassy slope above the rocks, and it first circled slowly round, then rose high and went away with a swift strong flight towards the Atlantic.

We wrote to the officer on board the *Caronia* in whose charge it had been. He replied, delighted with the news about Charlie, which was the name they had given it, and wrote, "Strangely enough on the day you liberated him the *Caronia* was passing quite close to the Cornish coast on her westbound passage to New York, perhaps Charlie saw her?"

Another great shearwater, who had this time crashed onto the deck of the *Queen Elizabeth*, was also sent from Southampton, and did not have such a happy ending despite all our efforts. She did not regain strength quickly, as Charlie of the *Caronia* had done, but when, after ten days, we decided to release her, she was eating enormously and had great power in her wings when we held her aloft.

A fine day came with a fresh wind, so we took her to the cliff, but she would have none of it, and ran swiftly over the turf, hiding in a hole, and we had to bring her home again.

Six weeks after her arrival, at about 9 p.m. one evening in September, she made an extraordinary cry, which sounded like a donkey's bray arranged by Malcolm Sargent; then repeated it four times. She did this all over again in the morning. Feeling this might be a call to her own kind we again took her to the shore, but once more she turned her back on the sea. She could not make it.

She stayed with us very content, and enjoying her food until eleven months later when she died in her sleep.

We had a bitter disappointment, too, with a Manx shearwater which was brought to us badly oiled and died four and a half months after his arrival. He was the first of his kind we had ever seen and was much smaller than the great shearwaters, but more than twice the size of the tiny storm petrel. His plumage was dull black above, with white underparts.

We made a special contact with this bird, and all the time he was with us we were struck by his amazing strength of will. He knew no fear, and gave shrill cries and whistles whenever he wanted anything. Every afternoon we had him free in the sitting-room and he climbed on the couch, and up on the arm of the chair on which we were sitting, staying there preening his feathers.

Everything to him was an adventure which must be pursued to the end.

We were planning his release; his feathers were perfect, and gleaming new ones had replaced those destroyed by the oil. Then, for no reason that we could discover, he suddenly weakened and died. When he made his last "flight" I held him aloft and as his wings spread out and moved fast it seemed that his game little spirit was really flying from his body. Afterwards, he folded up, as it were, breathed gently for a moment and lay still in my hands.

*   *   *   *   *

A real "problem bird" was a fulmar petrel. These birds are very remote from humans, being birds of the ocean and only returning to the shore for breeding purposes. They are rather like, but slightly smaller than, the herring gull, and differ from them greatly in their flight, which is of a gliding nature, continuing for long spells with only occasional beating of the wings. They have strange tubular nostrils as do all the petrels. Most peculiar of all is the habit they have of sometimes discharging from the mouth, with some force, a yellow oil, which has a strange sickly-sweet smell. (The aroma emanates from the body of the bird as well.) The reason for this is not definitely known, though sometimes it is done as a defensive action.

This fulmar that proved such a problem was brought to us one July. He was seen by two Mousehole fishermen not far from the Mousehole cave above which fulmars had first been known to breed only a few years before. They saw him, as they thought, having a bath as gulls often do, ducking his head and flapping his wings on the water. But when this went on for nearly an hour in the same spot they imagined the bird must be caught in a net or crab-pot line and took their boat over to release him. They found he was completely free, but utterly exhausted and water-logged; so they took him on board and brought him to us. They told us the bird had covered their clothes with a strong-smelling fluid, discharged from the mouth, when he was forcibly held. Whether he had thus used up all his supply of the secretion, I do not know; but we saw no evidence of any more until much later, in September (see note at end of chapter).

When the bird was handed over to us he behaved like a maniac, refusing all food, hurling himself about, and only lying still when left in a darkened place quite alone. However, after three days' forcible feeding his plumage looked perfect, especially his head feathers which were so silky and glossy white that we called him The Red Dean. His strength and balance seemed good so we decided to try a release. Knowing that fulmars are strange birds we felt nature might give him a better chance than we could.

We released him where fulmars are known to breed, near where he was found, and he appeared to be flying most strongly. But when a little way out over the sea he planed slowly down to the surface and once more the distressing business of ducking his head and flapping his wings began. He drifted slowly shorewards so we had to bring him back again exhausted and waterlogged.

This time he settled down at once and in a week was feeding himself; but as he walked about we saw his balance was very bad, just as before, although this did improve later with special capsules from the vet and plenty of raw egg. We wrote to expert ornithologists for advice but no-one could suggest a cause or cure; though James Fisher told us of a similar case, I believe in America, where the bird drowned, as ours would undoubtedly have done had not the fishermen rescued him.

In a month after his return The Red Dean was eating so well and looking so good we tried him out in our biggest pool. He swam around, seeming to enjoy it and returned to the bank to preen his feathers. Then he went back of his own accord into the pool. Almost at once he began to duck his head and flap his wings on the water. Realising that this was the end of our hopes, we took him out; once again exhausted and waterlogged.

When he was dry his plumage looked beautiful and continued to do so. His appetite never failed and he would eat up to twenty sprats a day. He drank a good deal, but we never again let him immerse himself in water, it seemed fatal to him.

He lived with us eight months in all, apparently quite satisfied with life, until he quietly passed away the following March. At his death the post mortem showed nothing to account for his original illness or for his death.

FURTHER DETAILS OF THE FULMAR PETREL'S BEHAVIOUR, TAKEN FROM RECORDS KEPT AT THE TIME

15 September. Throwing straws over his shoulder and digging in earth as if thinking of a nest. His feet have been peeling off old skin and his flight feathers moulting.

The Cry of a Bird

20 September. He spits at me for first time—a deep yellow colour. His flight feathers are beginning to grow and the plumage is looking better altogether. Seems now to eat heavily one day and starve the next. Very few droppings on the day he fasts.

19 October. Refuses to eat at all for five days but drinks heavily each meal-time, seems quite well otherwise. At the end of five days eats steak pie from my hand and goes back to normal feeding.

29 November. Tries to get out of run—find him with his head and neck under the door—not eating again but drinking heavily—preens his feathers, and seems very lively.

5 December. Eats again.

6 January. He spits at me (a yellow fluid) for second time. Having sprats daily which he loves.

8 January. Throwing straws over his shoulder.

20 January. He spits again twice, with great violence—think he has decided the box is his nest as each time he does it from there, in defensive attitude.

26 January. He emits the yellow fluid again. This fluid now comes more readily and more of it since the sprat diet (about twenty sprats a day).

10 February. Getting new tail feathers and head is white and glossy. Still eating sprats with great appetite and spitting yellow fluid, which, since sprat diet, smells just like sardine oil—before, it had a sickly-sweet smell, a bit like a flower.

1 March. Can get no more sprats and he goes off his food—only eats bits and pieces and does not enjoy it properly—does not spit any more.

25 March. Seems as if one leg is stiff—very cold weather so bring indoors—leg gets normal again, but he does not look well, and refuses all food—drinks heavily.

26 March. Give spoonful of raw egg and drops of halibut oil, and vitamin tablet—but he does not progress at all.

30 March. Can see he is quietly fading out so do not feed. He dies at 11 a.m.

Send for post mortem report which shows nothing to account for illness or death.

44

Chapter VI

A DOG POSSESSED

IT is strange how often a time of quiet and peace can be followed, out of the blue, by one of turmoil and unrest.

Pog and I used to welcome a "plain bit of life", as we called it, with no crises or problems in sight. It often came in the fall of the year when all the baby birds had been launched in the world, and our working day had settled into a busy but placid rhythm; or again in early spring with winter past, its gales and storm clouds forgotten.

We were enjoying to the full a day such as this one springtime. It was April: "All's right with the world", seemed written in the dew of early mornings. Then the turmoil returned.

A friend of ours had come for a holiday to Sennen Cove, bringing with her a perfectly ordinary young pedigree Airedale. He was straight from the kennels, so they were complete strangers to each other. For the first week she concentrated on getting to know Bob, as he was called, and found he was quiet and affectionate, and with no sign of nerves. Then this April day, she rang us up imploring our aid, and telling us what had happened.

Apparently all had gone well for the first week; then one morning, on being let out as usual, Bob failed to return. She went to look for him at midday and saw him on the cliff; he hesitated on hearing her call, and then bolted. She was naturally disturbed and finally felt desperate, as Bob fled at the sight of all who tried to help her catch him.

Days went by; he was seen by others in the distance, but fled instantly when approached. He must have been terribly hungry but the food she put out was never touched. Then he was seen no more by day, but reports came of a strange dog who roamed the cliffs by night, allowing no one to go near him.

It was at this stage that our friend asked us to go to help. She had evidently reached such a pitch of nervous prostration that we felt she was in no fit state to carry on. So we suggested her returning home to London, and leaving things to us. She was most thankful to do this, and gave us a free hand to act as we thought best.

We at once got down to devising a plan of campaign. We realized it would be a dusk to dawn job as Bob now only came out by night. Of course we could not both leave the birds at the same time so we decided we must tackle this new problem in shifts, taking it in turns; one of us to be at Mousehole (with the birds) and the other at Sennen (with the lost dog). We would just have to live from day to day, and night to night, having no idea how long this new job was going to take.

Pog went over that first evening at sunset, cycling the seven miles to Sennen. I was to relieve her the following evening.

When nightfall came, and all was still and deserted, she began to patrol the cliffs. It was during these solitary hours that one realized the mysterious, brooding atmosphere of that remote bit of Cornwall. By day one is struck by the beauty of the surroundings, the shining sands, and the blue-green colour of the sea. But when the light grows dim, haunting thoughts come of the wreckers of olden days, and of all those lives lost in the dangerous seas. Hanging over the desolate land is a sense of foreboding and doom. All that night Pog wandered over the rock-strewn track calling to Bob as she went. She saw nothing and heard no sound until after midnight, then a short distance away against the starlit sky, a dark silhouette appeared, only to vanish as she spoke his name, as suddenly as it had arisen out of the night.

Calling him seemed no good, so Pog thought the time had come to use a silent way of attracting Bob, one she had put off trying as long as possible. She took from her rucksack a parcel of raw liver. With this she lined her shoes, hoping so to lure him within reach. Such methods we were told, dog-stealers had used.

Now all was silence save for the revolting squelch from her shoes. But all to no avail, he remained a shadow dog. Although she sometimes heard padding steps in the darkness, he disappeared at the slightest movement from her.

Next day she spent at the village in the cove, trying to find out where Bob had last been seen. She followed up various rumours all leading to nothing, and it was impossible to discover where he lay hidden while daylight lasted.

That evening I cycled over from Mousehole, when the day's work with the birds was finished, and took Pog's place. She returned to Mousehole for a good night's rest so as to be ready for another strenuous day.

We both found the ride back a great refreshment, as this Land's End corner of England never looks more beautiful than in the fading light, with the line of hills dark before the setting sun. The winding lanes, with flower-strewn hedges, giving forth a mystical sense of fragrance from this dimly seen beauty. One becomes aware of this most fully when alone at the closing of the day. We scarcely ever met a soul as we rode back along the unfrequented by-ways.

This routine we repeated for many days. But by now people were getting alarmed at the thought of this semi-wild creature roving, without control, about the district, and we began to dread that Bob might be shot.

As a last hope we decided to get in touch with the kennels about forty miles away, where our friend had originally bought the dog. So we telephoned to the woman owner. She told us that it was John, her small son about eight years old, whom Bob had loved best; and that he would be far more likely to attract the dog back than she would. Without any hesitation she proposed letting the boy join us in our search. We told her it was a night job, but that did not disturb her, and they arrived together the following evening at Sennen.

Having talked to us she said she was quite happy to leave John with us at the fisherman's cottage where we were staying. He was an unusual child. His slender form and alert sensitive face made us wonder at first if we were going to ask too much of him. But he seemed to feel completely at home with us both from the very beginning; and soon showed us the stuff he was made of. He entered at once into the spirit of the adventure, and had an unshakable belief that Bob would come to him.

Now, from midnight onwards either Pog or I patrolled the deserted cliffs with John. Nights passed, and the boy's shrill treble voice echoed through the darkness, calling, calling, calling. The dog's dark image sometimes appeared, several yards away, but passing so swiftly there was scarcely time to be aware of him before once more he dissolved into the black night.

The days passed by. John played on the sands in the morning, slept in the afternoon, and later we kept our watch. At last Bob did seem to be coming nearer, and it was possible sometimes to hear the pad of his paws. Then one night the rattle of a dustbin was heard, coming from the courtyard of our cottage. This gave us the idea of trapping Bob in the yard. Next day was spent blocking up every possible escape route, leaving only the entrance open. It had no door, but we found an old iron wire mattress which exactly fitted over the opening. We filled a pail with liver and meat and put it in the yard as far as possible away from the doorway.

Our sister Mary came over to give us a hand, and we asked the sturdy fisherman, who was our landlady's husband, to stand by in case of need.

That evening we made a bed for John at the far end of the big porch, rolled him up in rugs and promised to call him if Bob should come.

Then the vigil started. It was a still night, the moon was coming up, a few clouds cast shadows on the cliff as we watched, in absolute silence, from the hidden shelter of the porch. The air seemed alive with minute sounds, but not the one for which we were waiting. At last, around two o'clock, we heard the now familiar padding feet coming nearer and nearer, then, an awful pause; we held our breath, the steps came on and a dim form stealthily passed into the darkness of the yard doorway.

Moving as one, the three of us rose on bare feet, making no sound, then clamped the iron bed-spring against the opening, holding it with all our strength. Hardly was it in place before Bob, a giant wolf in the half-light, hurled himself against the barrier. It shook, but held. Then came the appalling cry of fear when he found that he was trapped. He raced in circles round and round his prison, letting forth howls as of one possessed.

Now had to come the supreme test. We called to John, who jumped out of bed, quite undaunted by the unearthly cries, and came and stood between us. Without a shadow of fear he piped up, "Come on, Bob, good old Bob, it's your John, Bob," over and over again. In a few moments the howl ceased, the racing became an uneasy lope, the lope a tired pacing which finally halted a yard from the barricade.

Then the child acted. What possessed us I do not know, but we did not interfere. John put his hand round the side of the iron mattress, calling all the time in a very loving voice. The dog came calmly, and slowly, towards us. John stroked his head. The spell was broken, if such it had been.

We took down the barrier; John's hand fondled "his Bob"

who came quietly with us into the porch. He seemed very tired, and after a drink of water, he lay at our feet and put his head on my lap. We were all near to tears, even our fisherman friend. John was drowsy but happy; he tumbled into bed and was soon lost to the world. Bob stretched out, sighed deeply and slept.

The next morning we took him back to Mousehole, where he and John played in the garden all day.

Our friend came down from London and took Bob back to her own home, once more a happy, but unemotional, Airedale. He lived to be nearly thirteen, and never showed the slightest memory of those demented days and nights.

CHAPTER VII

DIVERS FROM THE DEEP

AFTER this strange interlude it was good to get back again to
our usual life with the birds. In a few days a new experience overtook us; it was the arrival of our first gannet.
Only the sight of the living bird could give a true picture of his
solemn beauty and silent dignity. The wonderful creamy-white
plumage shading to buff on the neck and head, and his great wings
tipped with black, were so impressive that we called him
Lohengrin.

He was brought to us by some men who found him lying in a
very weak condition on the Mousehole rocks, near Penlee lifeboat
station, and appeared to have no injury to account for his having
been stranded on the shore. After a few days of careful feeding he
was much stronger and eating three or four pilchards at a time,
which he took quite gently from our hands. One day through my
own clumsiness, he caught my hand instead of the fish I was
offering. I shall never forget the sharpness of his double-edged
beak which, in a second, had given me a bracelet of blood.

For two and half weeks he progressed well, and began to stand
up and stretch his wings. Then we noticed his left leg seemed to be
causing discomfort, and he went off his food. One evening, a few
days later, his appetite returned, but we saw with dismay about
half an inch of wire protruding from under the left wing. Next
morning it was sticking out an inch further, and although it did
not seem to distress him, we instantly consulted the vet who
thought the only thing to do was for him to try to remove it,
and took the bird to his surgery. We rang up in the evening to hear
how things had gone, and he told us a piece of wire a foot long had
been successfully removed; but the bird was said to be going on
well, so we felt more cheerful. Next morning we heard the sad
news that Lohengrin had died during the night. A post mortem
was made which showed there was a bad internal abscess, so I
suppose nothing could have saved him.

Gannets, to us, will always be "Birds of the Ice Age" because of their impersonal glacial eyes which hold a curious remoteness in their gaze, combined with a piercing scrutiny. Once they get over their initial bewilderment at the strange surroundings when brought to us, they settle down well, taking little notice of onlookers, and accepting fish from the hand as Lohengrin did. They object only to being moved around or held forcibly; all birds, of course, hate this, but to gannets it's an outrage. When cleaning them of oil (and gannets, like other diving birds, suffer so much from this) we try to work with the utmost speed so as to make the indignity last as short a time as possible.

After Lohengrin, three more gannets were soon brought to us which we called Tristan, Siegfried, and The Erl King. A young German student was up here one day looking round, and his face lighted up with surprise and pleasure on hearing these names. A fourth one which came later on was an especially enormous bird and we called him Olaf the White; he was found grounded in a field, very wild but with no injuries. After a few days' rest and good food we took him to the cliff edge where he stood inflating, flapping his terrific wings and then took off, a truly magnificent sight.

One August some visitors at Sennen Cove had watched a gannet badly oiled on one side lying helpless all day on the beach, and did not know what to do until someone told them of us. We thought they were the "right kind of people" because before bringing him they had wrapped him in their beautiful car rug, regardless of the oil.

We were so glad when the bird (which we called The Viking) rewarded them by doing an extraordinary thing. We had put him on the floor of our sitting-room. He could hardly stand for weakness but managed to swallow a pilchard; then he slowly climbed on to a low fireside chair, settled down on the soft cushions, took a tired look at us all with his spectacular ice-cold eyes, turned his head over on his back and went into a deep sleep. His rescuers were so pleased; they said it was the first time all day he had looked content. We carried the chair out to the run, and left him in it still sleeping soundly. He awoke in about two hours, took more fish and soon looked better. We did not attempt to clean him till next day; he was obviously too tired to stand any more. Once cleaned he got on well, and a month later was flying up on top of his house in wonderful condition so we decided to release him.

This is always a difficult decision to make for the diving birds, as the only real test of readiness is freedom itself. The birds seemed to know if we had not kept them quite long enough and they returned to shore and looked to us to "take them home". This did not often happen because we tested them out in every way we could before releasing them.

The Viking took off beautifully but we were a bit worried because when he was about two hundred yards out, instead of flying high and off, he flew low, alighted on the sea and swam along making no attempt to rise again. We left him then, hoping for the best.

Three hours later some Mousehole boys arrived with The Viking wrapped up in one of their coats. They said they were fishing just off the harbour when they noticed this bird swimming round and round their boat getting nearer all the time; finally it came and tried to get on board. They put a coat over him, helped him in and made for harbour. They then brought him straight to us. The Viking had returned from sea in a ship, truly we had named him well. Next morning he looked beautiful but was evidently not ready to go.

We kept him for nearly a year, happy and well. At the end of that time "The Snow Queen", another oiled gannet, was clean and ready for release so we took them together to the rocks, hoping she would guide The Viking back to his life at sea. All was well this time and they flew away with strong and confident flight (photos, pages 124 and 133).

Siegfried was another gannet who made a false start. He was brought to us one May from the North Cornish coast very badly oiled, but in a week we had got him beautifully clean (using chiefly lard and Lux).

After five weeks' convalescence he was flying up to the top of his house, and seemed ready to go. During this time we had sprinkled him daily from a watering-can to encourage him to preen his feathers and to keep him cool from the sun. Gannets never would go into our seabird pools, as the gulls so readily did; and as we could not enclose the Atlantic for their benefit, we had to resort to the watering-can. Fortunately this seemed to please them quite well.

When taken to the rocks for release Siegfried took off well, but returned to the shore after flying quite a long way out to sea. We left him on the cliff, and went down again in the evening. We found him still there, but he had moved to a different place, higher up.

The following afternoon he was still there, but after a time he spread his wings, made a very short flight, and dropped suddenly, falling into a cleft in the rocks from which it was very difficult to extricate him. We finally managed to get him up and brought him home.

After four more weeks with us he again got restless, so we made a third attempt at release. He took off well, flew strongly out to sea and was last seen heading towards the Lizard.

Three days later we had an S O S from the village asking us to come and rescue a large gannet lying by a boat in the harbour. We were quite sure it was Siegfried returned once more. He let himself be caught without any difficulty, and on getting home behaved just as before. He ate four pilchards straight off, but had some difficulty in swallowing.

We kept him six months this time, and then, in January, we let him go; with wild winds and rough seas he seemed in his element at last and flew strongly and well. No turning back this time, and we saw him no more.

One October a fisherman found a young gannet floating out at sea, too weak to rise though apparently uninjured. He took the bird on board and brought it to us. He was fully grown, a gigantic size, but still in his young plumage, dark brown speckled with white. We put him in front of the kitchen fire, but he seemed semi-conscious and would not eat for himself. On the fourth day when we went to feed him he stood erect, head upstretched, and transfixed us with such a stern judicial look that he had to be called "The Lord Chief Justice".

In a week he had found his voice, giving us a caution when fish was not to his liking. In three weeks his strength was enormous and his appetite terrific; his menu now was:

Breakfast	4 pieces of cod
Lunch	3 herrings
Tea	3 pilchards
Supper	4 pilchards
Bed-time snack	1 pilchard

We found he liked to stoke up one day and then eat very little the next, so the day before we released him we denied him nothing. To quote the records:

The Cry of a Bird

"*29 October*. A perfect day, calm on the sea, a little breeze, warm and sunny. We went down to the Cracker Rocks. When the carrying box was opened The Lord Chief Justice took his time, turned round to face us with a deliberate look (we hoped the summing-up was in our favour) and slowly made his way to the sea, launching himself in impressive style. He swam around enjoying his freedom for about twenty minutes then rose on his huge wings and flew away with amazing speed and strength, southward to the horizon. A wonderful transformation from his weak state of three weeks ago."

We wondered if the original trouble was that he had stunned himself in a high dive and so had been unable to get food; he was certainly in the last stages of exhaustion when found.

*   *   *   *   *

One memory that will always remain vividly with us is that of a great northern diver. These large birds of the far north are most beautiful and elegant with exquisite even white markings on blackish feathers tinged with a purple-green gloss. Their throats are ringed with two bands of white on a dark background which sometimes seem to flash like diamond necklaces. Their eyes are a curious deep red and shine like rubies, especially in some lights.

This bird was sent by the St. Ives' police in a wooden crate with labels all over it, "Beware of the Beak". Opening it in some trepidation an enormous flapping diver leapt out giving a haunting, wailing cry. He was covered with oil, and in an awful state, with one foot so affected that the webbing had dried like parchment. Where to put him was the problem, as great northern divers are always on the wing or on the sea except for breeding time in their Icelandic or other northern regions.

Pog then had a bright idea. We carried him to the studio, covered an ancient divan with newspapers and hoped the hollows and undulations of the surface would give a certain "wavy" feeling beneath him. It suited, and he lay quietly, sometimes moving with frog-like leaps but never attempting to leave his couch. That first night he continued to let forth the sad banshee wails.

In the morning there was an appalling smell, the bird was looking in disgust at his droppings which had soiled his feathers in a way unknown at sea. He then deliberately looked at us, and I lifted him up gently, while Pog hastily cleaned his feathers and put new papers down. I then replaced him on the couch. He made no protest, accepting the service as his right, and we christened him The Czar.

This affair was repeated every morning, only now he awaited our arrival before beginning the performance. He got us so well trained that we could all three act simultaneously. So the hygiene of the shore replaced that of the sea.

His beak was sharp as a rapier but never once did he turn it on us. He actually rested his beak on our hands as we cleaned him, seeming to understand our purpose and followed our movements over his feathers. After five days' constant work on them all his lovely markings were beginning to show. The vet gave us special lotion for the hardened webbing on his bad foot, but it eventually split and dried up completely; the other foot was not bad. He began to eat well; we taught him to take whole fish out of a deep pail of water held level with the edge of the couch.

Just nine days after The Czar came I was awakened at midnight by voices under my window calling, "Can you do with a northern diver?" I looked out and saw friends from Newlyn nearby, holding a large fish basket covered with sacking which heaved and rose with the violent movements of the diver within, accompanied by the terrible wailing cry.

Pog, who had been sleeping in the garden, was only half awake and heard the din as in a nightmare. We took the bird up to an empty run. He was as big as The Czar but in young, very dark brown plumage, and baby fluff still on his head. He hurled himself about with toad-like movements on his short legs, all the time wailing with dreadful grief. He had no injury and no oil on him; apparently he had been all day in Newlyn Harbour, but no one had been able to get near him until very late when our friends managed to throw something over him, get him in the basket, and so to us.

In the morning he had subsided slightly but was still very sad, so we thought the only thing to do was to get The Czar to the rescue. We put them in the run together, and instantly the young one stopped wailing. In a great leap he was beside The Czar who let him nestle down and began to preen his feathers in a loving way. Next he showed the young one how to take fish from the pail of water.

We called the newcomer The Midnight Son as they behaved as if they were a real parent and child. The Czar no longer gave his plaintive call, neither did The Midnight Son; calm and happiness prevailed. They were in a run with a large pool but they would never go in of their own accord. Twice a day at least we placed them on the water, and they swam and paddled around and waited for us to place them back on their grassy bed (photo, page 112).

We told the South Kensington Museum of the appearance of The Czar in May, because at that time it was thought the great northern diver never came south at breeding time. To quote the records:

"*3rd June.* I write to Guy Dollman who is working at South Kensington Museum telling of The Czar and subsequent arrival of The Son. He is polite and sceptical as are the ornithologists he consults. Finally they have to be convinced by a photograph we took as to the identity of The Czar but The Midnight Son they will not accept as being a young bird."

From now on the two birds progressed daily. The Czar's plumage was looking beautiful, the underdown growing again all over his skin. The Son was unmistakably getting adult plumage and the circlets were beginning to show round his neck.

At the end of June it seemed the time had come to release them. The Son was perfect, fully grown, fat and strong and we hoped he would encourge The Czar to make a bid for freedom. We rang up our Newlyn friends, the ones who had rescued the Son just a month before, and told them the great day had come, and they joined us. We put the two birds in a strong carrying box; it was a fearful minute when we closed the lid, but they behaved with majestic calm.

Pog and one of the friends went down to a lonely part of the rocks in case the birds should return to land; and the other friend and I carried the box carefully down to the harbour where a fisherman awaited with his motor boat. We boarded The Czar's launch and off. When opposite Pog on the rocks, and a fair way off shore, the motor was stopped, the boat drifted in silence. I then opened the box and first lifted out The Czar and placed him slowly on the sea, then did the same with the beautiful Midnight Son.

They swam happily along, the sun shining, the sea dancing, the ecstasy of freedom regained. Then The Czar submerged, The Son followed; they surfaced again not far from the boat, stood on their feet, flapped their great wings, made small circular flights low over the water. They never went far off, and it seemed as if The Czar was putting its child through its paces.

After watching them for nearly half an hour we returned to the harbour. We then went as quickly as we could down to the Cracker Rocks. This took us about twenty minutes. At the top of the cliff we were met by our friend who brought the sad news that The Czar had returned to the shore. She told us that after our boat had gone, the two birds played and swam about for some minutes, but gradually came nearer to the rocks. When quite close The Czar suddenly gave his heartrending, wailing cry, repeating it several times. As it died away The Midnight Son rose slowly and strongly on the wing, gradually gaining height and speed and making his lonely way out to the distant ocean.

The Czar had fulfilled his destiny, launched his Son in the world, strong and beautiful; then he returned to us weary and exhausted, his job finished. We felt sure his first cry in the studio was a call to his Son to join him; and his last on the rocks had been a final farewell. He never uttered it again.

Pog picked him up in her arms as he washed in on the waves, collapsed and shivering. She kept him warm in the sun and when he seemed a bit better carried him home; a sad procession this time. Once back in the run he stood up, flapped his wings, and began to preen his feathers serenely.

For two more weeks he enjoyed his food, and his pool, until one morning he did not want his fish, remained quiet and still until the afternoon when death came most peacefully.

CHAPTER VIII

THE WAR YEARS AND AFTER

ALTHOUGH the war clouds were gathering, kind hearts still found time to rescue birds in trouble, and our lives became more and more engrossed in looking after them. Pog was now having to give up her own work as she could not find time to do both this and the birds. An artist friend of hers, Ruth Adams, became so worried about it that she made up her mind to approach the Penzance branch of the R.S.P.C.A. She did not tell us of her intention, but sent a cheque to the local hon. secretary of the Society asking her to give the money to us anonymously, stipulating it was to be spent on labour to relieve our work. This we did, and a helper came up from the village, thus enabling us to have many free hours until the money was spent.

We did discover eventually who it was who gave it to us. Ruth herself gave away the secret, by her embarrassment when we continually discussed with her the intriguing question as to who the generous donor could be. I think she was afraid we might start writing grateful letters to the wrong people, so had to give the game away.

This kind gift was reported to the Society's headquarters and they sent a representative down to see what we were doing and what our needs were. The result of this visit was that they gave us a weekly grant of 15s., to be used as we thought best.

Following this first introduction to the R.S.P.C.A. we later heard we were to have a further visit in June 1939, from a Colonel Stordy, the hon. veterinary surgeon to the Society, who was coming to make a more detailed enquiry into our work. He was most enthusiastic and sympathetic, promising to return in the autumn with the chief secretary of the Society when they would discuss how they could best help with much-needed improvements.

But the autumn brought the war and an end to our hopes.

With the war years difficulties and troubles came to us as to everyone else.

The great problem was getting food for the birds, but friends gave us their coupons for bread and no-one reported us for illicit deeds. We managed to get through in spite of having more birds brought to us than ever before.

If the sanctuary had more birds during the war, then Mousehole certainly had more children. In 1942, numbers of young evacuees were sent to the district and many from the poorest parts of London came to live in the village.

The local children were given a week's holiday in which to get friendly with the newcomers and to show them the "sights". We came under the latter heading, and one day a whole gang came up to visit us. We did our best to explain the why and wherefore of everything. They listened in silence.

Then one little girl piped up, "Any reward?"

"None whatever, except that you will have saved a bird's life," we told her.

A fat little boy with the look of a future city alderman then said solemnly, "A beautiful idea, I think, meself."

Amongst these evacuees was a poor-looking boy about ten years old with rather a sad, wistful expression, who seldom said anything, but he brought more birds than any of the others while they were here. It was he who came running up the hill one evening with a scarlet face and breathlessly said to me, "Please come at once and break a window to release a jackdaw." It seemed that one had fallen down the chimney of an empty cottage, that all the doors and windows were locked and fastened and the owner away.

"We'd better try to get the key," said I.

"It's the bird or the window and it *ought* to be the window," said the boy.

Completely squashed, I called Pog, knowing she would enjoy the job. Armed with a hammer she and the boy went off to strike the blow for freedom, and out flew the bird quite uninjured. Having broken the law and the window they proceeded to present the policeman with the bits, an apology and a promise to make good the window.

The same boy later brought a seagull that was in a very bad way. I could see there was no hope, and told the boy so; but pointed out that nothing could now hurt the bird any more.

The boy rebelled at the thought of death and said, "No! He must be called Strongheart."

The bird died in the night. Next day I met the boy running full tilt down the hill; he stopped dead: "How is Strongheart?" I told him he had died in his sleep. "Damn," said the boy and went on running.

In the old days, before the war, Belgian fishing boats used to put in to Newlyn harbour to get food supplies and to take shelter in sudden storms. When Belgium was occupied by the Germans it was probably because of their contacts here that these same fishermen brought their wives and families over to England for safety. Many came to Newlyn, and some on to Mousehole where they were made very welcome and happy. The Belgian refugee children also brought us many birds, and we had a Leopold, Louis, Onbertine and Ostend amongst our patients.

A man who had escaped from Belgium during the occupation, and came here to live, was out fishing one day when he saw a baby razorbill, floating out to sea, a forlorn bundle of downy feathers, no parents around, and presumably having fallen from a nest on the cliff. He had not the heart to leave her, so took her on board his boat and brought her to us. We kept her warm and fed her on tiny bits of fish and cod-liver oil till her true feathers came, then we took her daily down to a long pool on the rocks where she had her swim. The children soon found out and came to watch her progress. We called the pool "The English Channel" and named the places from Land's End to Dover, and Cherbourg to Calais. The excitement grew as daily she reached another "port"—a Belgian boy joined us, and we had to take in Ostend. We had called her The Maid of Orleans as she came on the day of that town's liberation. After six weeks she was swimming, diving, and catching fish, her feathers and wings fully grown, so we knew the day had come for her liberation, too. We took her in a boat to where she was found, and left her, hoping her own family would now find her again.

The early years of the war brought more oiled birds to us than we had ever had before, and in a worse condition. Then later the numbers began to decrease and in 1942 we actually had no oiled birds—the same thing was noticed by one of the lighthouse keepers at the Lizard and by someone else in North Cornwall. It was suggested that ships were being careful not to throw waste oil overboard, for fear of betraying their presence to submarines. But in April 1945 we had a sudden influx of guillemots and razorbills, the bay being dark with oil. No sooner had we cleaned and fed and dealt with one, than the children brought up others, some in a pitiable state. It was hard going, as over the Easter holidays fresh fish was terribly difficult to get. I shall never forget that Easter morning when eleven guillemots came and stood round me in a big circle as I cut up what fish we had, their trusting eyes fixed on me. The tragedy of Europe's refugees seemed very close, for like them, these birds were lost, starving and helpless. Some we saved and released later, others had a contented few weeks of life with us enjoying their food to the last; the very bad ones we destroyed at once.

During these years when enemy planes were zooming round and bombs sometimes dropping unpleasantly near, we had a special basket made for Ben, our old jackdaw, now twelve years old. When the sirens sounded we would put him in this basket which we called his "Air Raid Shelter" and keep him with us until the "All Clear" went. In the autumn of 1942 he spent much time sleeping in this special house in our big drawing-room window, although perking up at night for his late dinner of crisp bacon.

I turned on the wireless on the morning of September 3rd at eleven o'clock, the anniversary of the outbreak of war. The whole nation was at prayer. Ben was still sleeping, head under wing. At 11.30, our hearts full of sadness, we turned and saw he was lying quite still and we realised our Ben had flown at last.

We were getting used to mysterious sights and sounds in those years of war, but during the early summer of 1944 strange and extraordinary-looking craft passed frequently, almost secretly, across the bay. We wondered what it all portended. Then came the tremendous news of the Normandy landings. D-Day at last!

Soon after this we had brought to us a poor little wounded magpie, with twisted leg and wing, and bad breathing trouble. We called her Tricolour in honour of the flag soon to be unfurled once more over France. She put up a tremendous fight for life, and thanks to the vet's treatment, and our warm linen cupboard, she came through, to live a happy life with us for six more years, though her wings could never fly freely again as the flag had done.

The following summer was overshadowed by the passing of

Nigger, the jackdaw brought to us as a baby just ten years before. He had never lost contact with us though living freely in the wild for all those years. Every morning he would fly in at Pog's studio window about eight o'clock and have breakfast on her bed. This strangely happy and complete friendship lasted until one morning in July, when, instead of landing on the window-sill as usual, there was a flutter of wings as he tried to get to the sill but fell instead to the ground below. Pog ran out to find him lying with both legs bleeding and broken. He must have met with a terrible accident; how it happened we shall never know. He had just had strength enough to get to the window and safety. This confidence in us touched us deeply, and made hard the sad decision we had to take. We knew Nigger, who belonged to the wild and free, must never be allowed to realise what had happened. As Pog held him in her arms, fear seemed to leave him and he slept. Still lying peacefully in her hands, Nigger was helped to go into that deeper sleep from which there is no return. Though we had to sever the link of this bird's mortal life, he himself, by his supreme and unfailing faith in us, had woven a thread of gold which will never be broken.

*   *   *   *   *

With the return of peace and the lifting of the black-out it was easier to face the personal problems we were confronted with. Cherry Orchard was now too big for us, and too costly to keep up, so we decided to sell the house, and move into a small bungalow named Green Hedges, which our mother with great foresight had had built at the end of our land, just before the war.

We felt it was really more than we deserved to have this lovely little home all ready to step into. We had done our best to try to persuade mother not to build it, because we had so hated the idea of having the best and most "secret" bit of our garden inhabited by strangers, and we did not feel we wanted any more possessions.

She was determined, however, to spend £300 she had saved up on it, and to let it furnished to help out with her very small income. She knew, too, that when she died, and the money was divided between the three of us, we should have very little to live on apart from what we earned from our precarious occupations.

The War Years and After

When the day came to leave Cherry Orchard for Green Hedges we realized what a gem of an inheritance it was. Built high on the edge of the old stone quarry, which bounds our land at this point, there was an uninterrupted view of the bay and the opposite shore stretching far away to the Lizard. St. Clement's Island, once the site of an old chapel, now the habitation of hundreds of seagulls, lay just below us like a lion couchant, guarding the harbour and village. In the years to follow we would often leave our supper table to gaze spellbound at the sunset afterglow as it travelled in a blaze of colour round the bay. From St. Michael's Mount, whose rugged sides rise up from the sea to carry on its summit a magic castle of quiet beauty, on to Cudden Point, dark in shadow; then with translucent light changing from pink to primrose, and soft mauve to grey and finally losing itself in the haze of the Lizard headland.

From our southern window we looked down on the apple blossom in spring; below lay our little lawn with its lavender hedge. There is beauty in building on a hillside, for one has to level and build up in small terraces, joining them by winding paths and steps. We did most of this ourselves, but our old friend, Willie Moncton, made our lawn (photo, page 112).

He had been employed for most of his life by the Mousehole builder who had built Cherry Orchard for Mother, the studio for Pog, and Green Hedges where we now hoped to end our days. Willie Moncton had helped in all this work, so it was to him we turned to add the final touches to our new home and garden.

He built a rough granite wall to support the lawn, levelling the ground with earth he dug out from the foundations of Green Hedges. He was always accompanied by his dog, Sausage, a great personality like his master.

This old friend of ours was a real craftsman, who loved and understood the material he worked in. Each piece of granite was used only when he knew it was "right" for the job. He told me how his father had taught him to "see" the stone in its place before it was actually put there; if it had to be discarded for another after having been set in position, it was bad workmanship. He became so absorbed in the building of a wall that his wife had sometimes to fetch him home to dinner. We felt the garden belonged to him as much as to us, he had put so much of himself into it. His love of flowers was very great. Once

63

when he and his wife were having tea with us on the lawn I pointed out some columbines and said, "They are like fairy flowers."

He fixed me with his very blue eyes and answered, "Miss Dorothy, they *are* fairies."

Well, we had solved our own housing difficulties, but not so those of the birds. As we looked forward to 1946 we could see nothing but grim prospects ahead. Our bird troubles, as usual, reflected those of the human world—food and housing being the most formidable. We took what reasonable provision we could as to the former, but the housing problem appeared insuperable.

After five years of war and enforced neglect of repairs, our main hut was daily becoming more of a wreck and the gales had worked havoc with the runs. The future seemed dark. Then we had a letter from the R.S.P.C.A.; they had not forgotten us, and were sending someone down to look into our difficulties.

After the visit things looked brighter. The Society now renewed its promise to bear the cost of improvements and generously raised our weekly allowance to £2, which was a tremendous help in meeting our evergrowing expenses. We then had the words "Assisted by the R.S.P.C.A." added to our board over the gate at Green Hedges. We were of course still doing all the work ourselves.

Our outlay consisted not only of fish and food bills, but medicines, veterinary accounts, carriers' bills, pots and pans, broom and dustpans, cement and sand, paints, nails, screws, hinges and all the hundred and one separate items which are needed when one tries to "do it oneself". Also there were telephone calls, telegrams and postage connected with the work.

As well as all this we had somehow to find money for our own equipment: rubber boots and oilskins, etc. We were always thankful for any old discarded mackintoshes to help out, as all-weather work is distinctly hard on clothes.

The number of bird patients rose each year; the need for our work seemed definitely established. The next struggle was to overcome the difficulties of post-war scarcities, permits and labour shortages. Our first target was cement instead of mud in the seagulls' runs, also watertanks and hosepipes instead of having to slop about with pails of water carried up from the

Cherry Orchard rainwater tank. Our only regret was that the seagulls did really prefer the mud, so we tried to introduce some by giving them tussocks of grass.

Winter, with more frustrating delays, was on us before the new hut for the little birds was even begun. However, those birds being unaware of the glories in store for them made cheerful song and murmuring conversations, bearing no grudge for the squatters' quarters they had to occupy.

The following year of 1947 began with bitter cold, raging gales and blinding snow. A tragic time for the wild birds, and non-stop work for us. As the frost continued, the number of half-frozen, starving birds found by the children increased—red-wings and starlings chiefly.

Every available bird house was full; at night the starlings would come and tap with their beaks at the lighted window. When it was opened they stumbled over the sill and the earlier arrivals moved along the perch to make room for the new-comers. All wild life seemed united in the face of the relentless cold. Many were too far gone to save; these we put in baskets near the slow warmth of the fire. A great peace seemed to enfold them and death came quietly as they slept.

The crisis for us came when for three days the three-mile road to Penzance was frozen over and all traffic stopped, which meant no fish for our sea birds. For two days we managed on our reserves; then Pog made a sleigh and trudged off the three and a half miles on foot. She returned triumphant with a wonderful haul, as our thoughtful fishmonger had saved up all our ordinary supplies.

The snow had frozen on the top of the wire-netting runs making them into kinds of igloos, and our beautiful white gulls looked positively dirty against it. We had to tie sacks on our feet to prevent slipping and went about with a hammer cracking up the ice on the pools, melting it down in pails on the stove and returning it to the baths, as our water pipes were, of course, all frozen. It nearly killed us seeing the gulls enjoying their icy ablutions, so cold did we feel. As someone in the village said to me in an affronted way: "We are not *used* to it down here."

At the height of the frost Pog had to share her studio with the birds. She left the window open all day with food and water inside. On the worst night of all, when she went in, from high up on the beams came the sound of a wonderful orchestra composed of

65

legions of starlings, rustling their feathers, chattering, trilling and whistling in every imaginable key. The iridescence of their plumage added spangles and jewels to the wonder of the music. Pog crept out in silence, so that not one performer was disturbed. The frost broke at dawn, and they gave her back her studio.

CHAPTER IX

LOVERS AND PARENTS

How we welcomed the following spring, and the re-awakening of all living things. Every year the birds became more a part of our lives and our awareness of them grew.

We saw how a bird's intensity of feeling for its mate awakens early in the year, and how differently each kind of bird expresses this feeling.

Two injured rooks, Rex and Rill, showed us the delicacy of their love-making. For some months they had been friendly with one another and then one Valentine's Day they celebrated with a "kiss". Slowly they approached each other with drooping wings and loving sounds, and then gently touched each other's beaks. From this time on their courtship gave them great happiness, but they were always dignified and deliberate, unlike the rude jackdaws with their over-excited tailwaggings and hot-headed behaviour. Some days later Rill displayed before Rex and began to feed him, and then they started to build a nest in the hut, but pulled it down again. In April, they built another one in the run, Rill doing most of the work. Two weeks later we found a blue speckled egg on the ground, but as far as we could discover they had no more.

After a happy summer together Rex died; he had always been the weaker bird, possibly owing to the bad injury he had when brought to us. Rill completely recovered from her broken wing, and was in perfect plumage when a few weeks later she flew off confidently and well.

Francesca, a great black-backed gull, had three husbands during her life with us. She was faithful to each one until they died, or became too old to be interested in her; and only then did she console herself with a new lover.

Francesca will always be remembered by us for her contented, placid nature, so unlike the usually aggressive members of her tribe; also for the length of time she spent with us—seventeen years in all.

She had been brought in originally with a torn muscle, and a nasty wound on the shoulder of her wing, which was hanging badly. The injury must have happened some days previously, because the flesh was full of maggots. We soon disposed of these, and healed the wound; but the wing would never go into full stretch again. Twice we tried her outside, but she seemed to know she could not make it, and returned of her own accord to the run.

She mixed freely with all the smaller herring gulls, but never molested them. In fact she kept such good order that we nicknamed her The Mother Superior (photo, page 93).

Then, one day, a newly-arrived great black-backed gull, Kharkov by name, fell for her. She returned his love, although he was an old-looking bird and unable to fly. We gave them a run to themselves as he was paying her decided attentions, "kissing" her and preening her feathers continually and walking about with straws in his beak. In two weeks' time an egg appeared, but their mating must have occurred when no humans were around, because we had no idea the exciting event was to take place.

For years they enjoyed life together and eggs arrived each spring; but each time, after a few days, all we saw were shells. Kharkov, we suspected, was responsible. When the fifth spring came he no longer courted Francesca, but lived quietly to himself until he died two years later.

In the meantime a very large great black-back had come to us with a bad wing; we called him "Pluto". This time it was Francesca who made the advances and Pluto became her mate for two years. Again all was very discreet; the eggs came, but each year the husband disposed of them.

When he died she took to herself her third, and last, mate, an enormous great black-back, Starlight. This time we actually saw the end of the eggs. Starlight was seen going very slowly towards the nest with gliding step and neck stretched to the full. Then he took an egg carefully in his beak, threw up his head and it disappeared at one gulp. Francesca showed no opposition whatever.

For the last two years of her life, after Starlight's death, Francesca lived in retirement. Her courting days were over.

She had lived happily with us for all these seventeen years, causing and giving no trouble. She was in adult plumage when she was brought to us, so she must have been at least twenty-one years old when the last call of nature came, taking her very quietly in her sleep.

Of all the birds we have had I think none could better qualify, as truly faithful lovers, than Rider and Hedger, two herring gulls (photo, page 54).

They came in 1943, Rider in September, Hedger in November, both war casualties, each with a wing completely severed at the shoulder. An airman told us this was often caused, much to the men's regret, by the bird flying against the wire of the practice target towed behind their planes.

Rider and Hedger, both first-year birds in speckled brown plumage, were put with many other herring gulls, but from the first they became friends. After their first mating, when five years old, they continued having eggs each year. Rider, the male bird, never touched the eggs, but we removed them, as we did all the other birds' eggs, after a week, so as not to increase the population beyond all bounds. However, one year we must have left one egg too long by mistake. When we went up to remove it we were greeted with a "cheep"! It was Empire day so we called the baby Empiricus.

At first the parents took the greatest care of him, and fed him well from a pan of specially nourishing food we gave them, in addition to their ordinary fish. In five weeks' time we found they were wolfing up the special food themselves, and leaving the baby to feed himself. A few days later we noticed his balance was bad; we decided it was lack of vitamins so separated him from his parents. After giving him a special diet he quickly recovered.

At this time we had another baby herring gull hatched out here, three weeks later than Empiricus. We called her Moo-loo after her parents Balloon and New Moon. When Moo-loo was four weeks old we put her with Empiricus in a special run where they played together with sticks and bits of wood, having numerous baths and looking completely happy. They grew into marvellous birds. Next we let them mix freely with some adult herring gulls who had recently been brought in from the wild, hoping the grown-ups would teach the young ones the ways of the outside world in order to prepare them for their release.

We let them go together when Empiricus was about five months old and Moo-loo about four and a half months. All was successful and they flew off with confidence, their flight strong and even. They often returned to the hospital for a feed, especially Empiricus, so we knew that all was well with them (photo, page 42).

Rider and Hedger, apparently, had no desire to mate after they were sixteen years old. They were then put into a run by themselves, where they sat, side by side, serene and happy, in beautiful plumage, enjoying their baths and food as usual. They are still here now, in 1961; eighteen years old (photo, page 54).

From what we saw of these two pairs of herring gulls it looks very much as if seagulls mate for life. Certainly in both these cases they remained completely faithful to each other even though they were in contact with many other herring gulls, and were quite free to make their own choice.

Francesca, also, mated every year with the same bird, until death or desertion through old age intervened. So it appears that great black-backed gulls are true to each other for life as well.

Neither the herring gulls nor the black backs seem to mate until full maturity of plumage is reached, in their fourth or fifth year.

* * * * *

The greatest lover of them all was Phoenix, our passionate wild rock dove, brought to us one May, a few days old, having fallen from the nest built over the cave in Mousehole cliffs (photo, page 72). Rock doves, with their distinguishing white rumps and black bars on their wings, still nested there at that time. His hunger was like a consuming fire. He rushed up and down on the window seat and would not stay still for a second, making it quite impossible to feed him. We did not then know that baby pigeons, unlike most birds, take the food *out* of the parent's mouth and do not have it pushed *in* by the parents. We had been trying to do just this, and everything was covered with milky mash. Pog had almost given up as a bad job, when Phoenix noticed that she was holding some food loosely in the hollow of her hand. He saw his chance and plunged his head into her hand, supping up the food in furious haste. Once again a bird had taught us the right way to go about things.

We continued to rear him in our sitting-room at Cherry Orchard, and by Valentine's Day the next year he was flying about freely inside and out but returning each night to sleep in the room until April, when he began to sleep out. He still, however, came daily inside to see us.

One day we saw him bring a small grey pigeon with him to our lawn and we suspected he was "walking out". In November, he succeeded in luring her into the sitting-room and we realised his intentions were serious. She was dainty and shy, and we called her The Dove.

They both now slept on a bough fixed in the room, with a basket nearby for a nest. Phoenix, however, did not think much of this idea, and when spring came, he started carrying sticks to the fireplace and building in the grate. We were not so keen on this project and put the material back in the basket. Next day he removed it all, this time to the coal bucket. Once more we were firm, but were struck with the coincidence of our "bird of fire" having chosen such sites for his nest.

In early summer we were expecting friends and I had arranged a special bowl of flowers on the table—roses, jasmine, honeysuckle and lavender. Just before lunch I went to see that everything was ready. To my horror, there was a trail of flowers all over the table, across the carpet, and finally on the black hearth rug where The Dove was sitting with bits of honeysuckle, jasmine and rose tucked in under her. Phoenix was walking round and round this exotic nest, cooing, sweeping the floor with his tail, and bowing his head before her beauty. Anything more exquisite I have seldom seen.

*   *   *   *   *

Another great romance was that of Truelove, a wild herring gull who fell in love (through the wire-netting) with one of our permanent inmates. She came daily one April, walking up and down outside the run close to the door, but taking no notice of food. One night, we found her scratching a nest on the ground beside the run, and the bird inside watching. Such devotion to a crock, with the whole world of perfect birds from which to choose, could no longer be ignored. We opened the door and in she went, welcomed by her expectant friend. They began to build a nest of sticks and straw, supplied by us, and three or

71

four weeks later Truelove laid two eggs. When she tired of this domestic life some weeks later, she went to the run door. We opened it and off she flew, but she continued to return from time to time for food all through the summer.

One May another pair of herring gulls were coming daily and carring off some of our early potatoes; then in June a boy brought a baby gull from the St. Clement's Island off Mousehole where he found it striding about, one immature wing hanging. We fed him on mashed fish and egg, the wing soon strengthened and he was big enough to go in the run. Almost at once, the two "Potato Gulls" as we called them, landed on the wire-netting and the baby called to them. They spent every day lying on the top of his run and one always stayed there for the night. As the young one always greeted them with a call, we felt sure they were his real parents, so called him The New Potato. In four and a half weeks he was looking wonderful, the wing absolutely recovered and when Mr. and Mrs. came in the morning we took the young one to the potato patch. The old gulls joined him and then kept all other birds off. They showed him how to fly up to the top of the run and from there they all took off together.

Five days later The New Potato came and sat beside Pog in the garden. After a feed, he settled down happily and did not move for half an hour. The Potato Gulls were on the roof but he did not join them, nor they him. We then put him back in his run where he had an enormous bath. A week later he rejoined his parents, coming back often for food but never inside again.

*   *   *   *   *

Lammas and Justine were a pair of jackdaws whose devotion was absolute. Lammas came with a hopeless wing. Justine's wing was also injured, but not so badly, and after three years she made a complete recovery, so we released her in August when courting time was over. We put Lammas in a new house to take his mind off things.

After three days Justine was back. She looked first in the old hut, and not finding him there she eventually discovered him in the new house. She could not get in, so returned through the open window of the old hut and waited for us to catch her.

Lovers and Parents

Their reunion was most touching. They "chucked" at each other, Lammas's head feathers rising with pleasure, Justine sitting closely beside him, preening his head and neck; not thinking of food or drink. To be with her loved one was the only thought in Justine's mind, so we let her remain, a voluntary inmate. They had eggs several times but they did not come to anything.

Five years later Justine was let out by mistake and remained away for ten days. But again love called her back. She insisted on being let in, and their mutual happiness was so obvious that we decided to let her stay. They had both been adult birds when originally brought to us, Lammas ten and Justine eight years before, so they were getting on in life.

Lammas died two years later; Justine, after having voluntarily renounced freedom for all these years, then flew off and this time did not return.

For fidelity both as lovers and parents, it would be hard to beat Neverest and Link, another pair of jackdaws. Neverest fell down a chimney as a baby, the same day on which Mount Everest was climbed, hence his name. Link, also a youngster, was found by a golfer on Lelant links some miles away. She had a damaged wing but it healed well, and we were able to release them both together in a few weeks. At first they came back to us each night to roost and to visit us by day; but by autumn were sleeping out.

Every morning, for the first year, they flew in at my bedroom window at Green Hedges to play about on my bed. Neverest, in particular, treated me like dirt, pushing bits of bread and butter (first stolen from my breakfast tray) under my pillow or into the neck of my pyjamas. They then extended their enterprising behaviour to the studio where they discovered Pog always slept; and she was now tormented in the early hours of the morning. Soon they began to explore the rafters and beams in her studio, roosting there often during the day and coming and going as they pleased.

This was how they lived until they were just two years old. Then, that spring, they began to carry sticks and bits of paper up to the beams where Pog hastily fixed a box for them. In two weeks eggs appeared. They sat in turns, one bird always flying off at night.

Three weeks later egg shells were thrown out and from the

nest came tiny sounds which soon developed into yells for food. The Golf Ball had arrived.

Either Neverest or Link stayed with the baby on the nest for four days and nights; then they both flew off each evening, leaving Pog to mind the baby till they returned to duty early in the morning.

In five weeks The Golf Ball was taught to fly about the beams, but was left alone at night, and obviously told not to leave the studio, though the window was always open for the parents to come and go. Seven days later they took him for his first flight outside; in the end he slept out too, but all three returned daily for food and a rest on the beams.

The following spring Link and Neverest flew up to their old nest on the beams, but finally decided not to build there. At the end of April, we saw Link in the garden looking ill, Neverest sitting beside her preening her feathers. He flew up to the studio window and called to her to follow. She made a short flight towards him and we saw spots of blood. She could not reach the window so we caught her and put her in the jackdaw hut, where Neverest joined her, constantly preening her feathers.

Next day she was very quiet. Not liking the look of her, we asked the vet to come and he feared an internal injury although she did not seem in pain. Neverest tended her with the utmost devotion, but she died that night in her sleep.

In the morning we opened the window. When Neverest was quite certain she was dead, he flew. He returned later to Pog's studio, but never went back to the hut.

The winter after Link's death, Neverest appeared at the studio one day with drooping wing, so we kept him in for some months until it strengthened. During this time he had enjoyed listening to the wireless. His choice of programmes were football matches, preferably Cup Ties, and church services—any denomination would do.

For the next two years Neverest remained solitary, then he consoled himself with Buttons, a smart young lady, younger than himself, who had been a patient but was now flying freely. She literally threw herself at him by forcing open the wire-netting which covered the studio window and joining him on the beams.

In the following April awful mating sounds were heard coming from the old nest which had been draped with new materials, and in early May two eggs arrived but did not hatch out. Since then they have stayed together, flying freely all day but usually returning to the studio at night to sleep.

Now, in 1961, Neverest is in his ninth year and Buttons about six years old, still true to each other.

Chapter X

FROM AIR, SEA AND LAND

As the years went by, we began to feel word must have gone around among the birds that they could come to us when in need of help, when food was scarce, or when some disaster had overtaken them. Some even came to die.

One of the first birds who discovered the sanctuary all by himself, was a herring gull. We found him crouching down outside one of the runs, very weak and evidently glad to be safe. We did our best for him, but on the fourth day he died. The post mortem showed heart trouble and anaemia.

The next bird that came alone was a blackbird, who was found sitting on the path by the raspberries. She did not move when approached. There was a small swelling under her right eye which was closed, and she let me pick her up without resistance. The vet came and found it was a kind of blood blister, probably the result of an injury. He carefully let the blood out and gave us a dressing for the wound.

Raspberry, as we called her, had no fear of us at all and fed from our hands. In two days her eye was showing a tiny bit; the next day it was half open and on the fourth day it was almost wide open. She was now feeding herself and beginning to go wild. It was interesting to notice how the lack of fear only lasted while the injury was at its worst; with each day's improvement she got a little less tame, and in ten days was absolutely wild when recovery was complete. We released her among the raspberries and she stayed about the garden all that summer, sometimes flying right across our faces. This is something that birds we have released often do; as if to attract our attention.

A chaffinch too came back to us of his own accord in time of trouble, having in the first place been brought to us one July with a damaged wing which had soon healed and he was set free. He returned daily, sometimes to feed, and sometimes just to greet us. One evening in September, instead of flying round he

76

hopped at my feet and stopped at the door of his old run. I then saw one eye was closed, a beadlike swelling over it. Without any difficulty I caught him. He was obviously pleased at being inside again. The swelling this time was a tick which fortunately fell off of its own accord. Once this had gone, his bright eye opened and in a few days he was able to leave, coming back to see us as before.

There was another young chaffinch who flew in at our open window one day and sat firmly beside the cage where we were rearing a baby sparrow. We were equally firm, and put her out of the window; but next evening she sat almost under my feet in the garden. Realising there must be something wrong, I brought her in and put her where she wanted to go, with the sparrow, and they were most happy together. In two weeks both were fat and well, so we opened their door and off they flew, coming back, still together, for many weeks just for a feed, so we knew they were safe.

One year an undersized and poor-plumaged young herring gull, who maybe had lost his parents, came on to the top of the run when he saw us feeding Dauntless and other wild gulls, all "outsiders", some not even ex-patients. But he never got a look in as the stronger birds chased him off.

One day he did not turn up; but at dusk, when the wild gulls had all gone off, Pog saw him floating silently down, following her movements, as she turned away thinking her day's work was done. She quickly collected some special bits of fish, and he had a glorious feed. Every evening the same thing happened, and Pog called this her "Appointment with Fear". All through that summer he came. By the autumn he was able to hold his own with the other birds, and the assignation became unnecessary.

An incident happened one day when we were having lunch on the lawn which might have had a disastrous ending. It was also a very unusual way for a bird to arrive. We suddenly heard a cry from a bird coming from the apple tree, and saw a jackdaw holding something. We shouted and clapped our hands and instantly the jackdaw flew away, dropping a robin which fell to the ground like a stone. Pog picked it up; it looked dead, but she felt a slight grip on her finger from one foot. I ran into the house and got a deep cardboard box and put a soft piece of blanket at the bottom of it.

Pog then carefully brought the box indoors with the bird still gripping her finger, but looking rather lifeless. Then she withdrew her hand, but, before I could get a cover on top, the robin suddenly "came to life", and shot past our faces up to the open entrance to our attic, immediately overhead. There he sat quite still and we also did not move. He then flew into the attic which extends under our roof and is completely dark, and full of every kind of lumber.

We knew there would be little hope of finding him if he should have another queer turn, so Pog crept up the ladder and finally located him sitting motionless on the top of a trunk. She crept back without a sound and we thought the only thing to do was to await events. So for nearly an hour we sat in view of the attic entrance, taking it in turns never to take our eyes off it.

Finally we were rewarded; Atticus, as we had now named the robin, silently appeared at the entrance, shook himself and flew in an unfaltering flight over our heads and out of the window. It was a complete recovery from what we thought must have been a real faint, from fright only. The jackdaw must have held him very gently because there was no blood on Pog's hand and obviously no injury to the robin's feet or wings.

Atticus has returned every day to our sitting-room ever since this episode. We know him from other robins which come inside by his rather faded coloration and from the fact that he always perches on the ladder going up to the attic.

Another gate-crashing patient was a great black-backed gull. He had been coming to the top of the run for food during a spell of very bad weather one February. We always knew him because one wing hung forward at the shoulder. On the ground he looked hopelessly disabled, but in the air he flew perfectly, so, whatever the original injury had been, it had mended without impeding flight.

One morning we found an extra black-back inside the run. We could not account for his presence until we looked up and saw an enormous hole torn in the wire-netting overhead. The bird must deliberately have forced an entry. We saw it was the one with the droopy wing we had been feeding outside, so we called him "Drop In". He stayed for two weeks, eating everything we gave him and enjoying his self-chosen confinement. Then came a change in the weather, a lovely day, and he showed us he would like the door opened; and off he went, confident and strong, and he is still coming, not every day, but quite often, sometimes bringing his mate with him. She is slim and elegant but shy of us and will not feed from the hand as Drop In still does.

January 1952 calls to mind Captain Carlsen and his valiant endeavour to bring his badly damaged ship, *Flying Enterprise*, safely to port at Falmouth. At this time a wild jackdaw was also fighting the elements, handicapped by an illness which was getting the upper hand. We had noticed the bird when he came to the studio window for food, as he had a small swelling under each eye. He was too wild to catch, but as the weather got worse he came to sleep at nights in the pigeon loft. Finally we managed to close the window with him inside. Had we not done so he would never have had the strength to make the loft again so weak had he become, and he now had a cough as well. This was the actual day that Captain Carlsen's great effort ended just across the bay. We decided this bird ought to carry on the name and that it would be up to us to help *our* Flying Enterprise to sail again on the wind. The vet came and gave various treatments, making an incision in each cheek to release the discharge; but they filled up again almost immediately.

Otherwise the bird regained strength very quickly with good food, and as the trouble was so local and he a perfect patient, we felt we must not give up.

Every night and every morning for every day of the year the bird sat quietly in our hands while we did the necessary dressings. The cough soon went, and a tick on the cheek was removed, but the discharge persisted in spite of medicines, penicillin, M. & B., golden eye ointment, etc.

At last it began to dry up; and, eighteen months from the day he came, The Flying Enterprise, perfect in plumage, healthy and strong, regained his freedom, flying high over the fields. Two evenings later we heard his voice in the loft but he never slept there again.

* * * * *

The wild birds who had made such a personal appeal for help were always given a responsive welcome by us. Nor could we refuse refuge to another wild creature which was brought to us in distress, although it could not qualify as a bird. It was a seal. We felt it had a claim on us because the heritage of the

Cornish coast belongs equally to the seals as to the birds; and seals can be seen on many a summer day, disporting their supple bodies in the sea, or sunning themselves on the rocks. On shore they look heavy and clumsy, but once in the water they follow the ceaseless flow of the waves, becoming lithe and graceful.

The call came to us from a pathetic baby seal. One rough November evening some boys were heard shouting out: "There's a seal by the harbour wall, Miss Gleeshus. We thought you ought to know." Pog took the broad hint and went to find a large crowd gathered, all wondering what to do. She took her coat, put it round the slippery body and a friend helped her to get it into a large fish basket. It was a terrific weight but with many willing hands they got it to the bottom of our hill. Then Pog told the boys to do a hold-up of the first car that came. They spread across the road and their fierce onslaught duly stopped one. The driver, once he understood the need, turned round and very kindly took Pog and her burden up to the studio.

Once there the seal quietened down and seemed to realise it was safe. It even took liquid nourishment from a spoon. The vet came and diagnosed pneumonia. The poor little thing was in a bad way, but it seemed to like Pog gently wiping away the discharge from its nostrils, putting its baby flippers on her hand as she did so. Everything possible was done, but it died the next day.

A few years later another seal was found washed up on the north Cornish coast, thin and miserable, again with a mucous discharge from mouth and nostrils; not a baby this time, but a young one not yet fully grown. When he arrived here the studio, as before, was the only place for him.

At first he was very wild and charged at us showing a fine row of teeth. His fierce ways earned him the name of Tiger. Then Pog fenced off a corner of the room, giving him a bed of straw, a warm blanket and a large low zinc bath, big enough for him to get into—although by the time he had wallowed in it there was more water on the floor than in the bath.

That first night it was rest, not water, he needed. When Pog went up later she found him lying on his back on his bed, his two flippers folded under his chin, in an absolutely blissful sleep.

Next day the vet came. He again diagnosed pneumonia and gave a penicillin injection. The problem now was how to feed

Tiger. He ignored fish thrown or handed to him, and just charged at us. Then Pog got a soft washing-up mop, soaked it in cod-liver oil, stuck a pilchard onto that, and this time *she* charged. Tiger was taken by surprise, he lunged at the mop, and swallowed the oil-soaked fish.

After a few meals like this he soon took fish from the hand without any trouble. The pneumonia responded to treatment; and as his health returned he consumed vast quantities of fish, growing daily in size and weight.

In a month his proportions were so enormous we knew we must act quickly and return him to the sea before he became quite unmovable. It took two strong men, the R.S.P.C.A.'s Penzance and Truro inspectors, to carry him in a large water tank from the studio to their car and then off to the north coast again.

On a sandy beach they rolled him out of the tank at the edge of the shallow surf. He took leaping plunges through it and out to the breakers beyond, returning to his wild life with never a backward look.

*   *   *   *   *

Although never a patient, there is one other animal whose story must be told—a lost dog who was brought to us and who became very much a part of the sanctuary. His strong and loving personality was felt by both the people and the birds who came into his life.

In August during a very hot summer a Swedish artist found this young collie sheepdog lying on the Mousehole rocks, too weak to stand, his ribs and backbone standing out in ridges from his starved body. We were fetched and Pog and a friend carried him up the hill to the hospital. We laid him on the lawn and felt sure he was dying.

The vet came, and he thought the dog must have run many, many miles to get in such a condition. He said he was not more than six months old, and might recover with proper nourishment.

We told the police and advertised him as "a dusky brown", etc., so the name Dusky came into being and with it the most wonderful dog we have ever known.

In two weeks' time he was quite fit, and not having discovered his owners we thought we ought to find him a good home.

He needed so much exercise; he was too young and we were too old.

A lovely home was eventually found for him with some people living six miles away. They came to fetch him in their car.

Ten days later, at seven in the morning, he was back on our doorstep.

His new master was anxious to have him again; and he came in the car, in the dark this time, to fetch him away.

A week later, again at seven in the morning, there was Dusky back on our doorstep.

He had chosen the "old sheep" he wanted to look after; and so he came permanently into our lives. We could not send him away after that (photo, page 93).

From the beginning he understood our work with the birds. We never trained him in any way, but when a bird was brought, he would run ahead, tail waving, showing the way to the runs. He appointed himself "the Hospital dog".

If he heard the warning cry of a jackdaw he would go like a streak from our doorstep, find the trouble (usually a cat), chase it out and return to his post; but he was a perfect gentleman over this, never touching the cat. One day we watched him from the window, chasing a cat down the path; when he got within a yard of it, he stopped and marked time, waiting for it to get ahead before he continued his round up.

The birds seemed to have no fear of Dusky. In fact, some of the young ones when flying freely for the first time would return to him rather than to us for protection, just as Piccadillo, the puffin, did.

One evening he was lying fast asleep on the couch and I put Coco, the shelduck (then only a week or so old), on the cushions while I cleaned out his house which was in our sitting-room. The telephone rang; it was a long call, and when I turned to put Coco to bed there was no sign of him. I searched everywhere, under all the furniture, under the cushions, and was getting really worried when I looked at Dusky, still fast asleep. There in the midst of his soft curled-up tail was Coco, very pleased at having discovered such a warm nest.

The nearest we came to discovering Dusky's place of origin was one night when we were listening on the wireless to Thomas Hardy's *Far from the Madding Crowd*. Dusky never took the slightest notice of radio sounds. Dogs could bark, horses neigh, cats fight and humans talk and sing; he slept through it all. This evening he was asleep as usual. Then Gabriel Oak in the play called out "Ovey, ovey, ovey" with a musical but rather mournful intonation. Instantly Dusky sprang from the couch, stood facing the wireless, ears cocked, tail alert, waiting for further instructions. We hated to let him down like this, so wrote to Paul Rogers, who had taken the part of Gabriel Oak, congratulating him on his interpretation as understood by Dusky and asking for help as to what to do next. Paul Rogers was most appreciative of Dusky's response to the call, but could not explain its meaning. Both he and the B.B.C. had been puzzled as to how it should be uttered. No-one could help him about this, he told us, so he thought back to his childhood days in Devon, and recalled the shepherd's cry; then he used this sound with Hardy's words. It looked as if Dusky was a Devonshire dog.

One summer we were so busy that we found it difficult to cope with visitors. So on those days when we were working long hours without a minute to spare, we put a little notice inside our gate, saying, "Very sorry, no time for visitors to-day." One such day we were having our supper around 9.30; it was a lovely summer evening, and still quite light. We heard Dusky's tail thumping with pleasure on the doorstep but no sound of voices or footsteps. A minute later we caught a glimpse through a side window of Dusky's tail waving in the air as he went up the steps towards the birds' enclosures, and behind him three or four young people, Indian file, all bent double, evidently hoping to keep out of range of the window. We did not want to spoil the fun, so waited to see what would happen.

After about fifteen minutes we heard whispered voices below our window saying, "Thank you, Dusky, dear, for showing us round"; they must have read his name on his collar. They then tiptoed off and he returned with a contented flop to the doorstep. When we asked him what he had been up to, he gave us a superior look, suggesting he knew how to behave even if we did not.

Dusky was nearly fourteen when he died, leaving a place in our hearts all his own.

CHAPTER XI

SOME UNUSUAL PERSONALITIES

ONE of Dusky's greatest friends was Santa Fé, the crow, who was found one May by the side of the main road, on the way to Helston. He was lying under a high tree at the top of which was a torn and ruined nest, and no parent birds were to be seen. A motorist saw the pathetic sight and could not pass it by. He saw that the bird had blood in its mouth, and was worried what to do with it. Then he remembered that when he was in the Far East during the war he had seen a film about a bird hospital in Cornwall. On making enquiries he found the address was Mousehole, and along he came.

Of all the ungainly babies this was the worst; long legs, goggling eyes and pathetic, hoarse cries. There was no more sign of any bleeding after he arrived; so we made a nest for him in our sitting-room out of a waste-paper basket, to which he became so attached that he would not leave it, even when he was fully feathered and well able to perch on a bough. It became a kind of complex, perhaps the result of his early bad experience. So we had to transfer him, nest and all, to the studio, which was the only place big enough for such a large bird to learn to fly.

This he did by slow stages, taking three times as long as Pepper, the jackdaw, before he finally had his first night sleeping out. In fact, we think it was Pepper who insisted on his doing this, as they always flew a lot together. They were also about the same age, and had been reared in the same room (with Dusky to mind them). Pepper first slept out on June 29th and never came back to sleep after that; Santa Fé had his first night out on August 21st, but continued to come back to roost inside again on and off.

One morning in October, Santa Fé returned very tired and excitable as if he had flown further afield and seen new sights. Pepper came with him but did not fly off until he had shown Santa Fé where to rest on the beams. The latter obediently went to the chosen place and slept soundly.

Some Unusual Personalities

The following January a large crow came to a tree in the garden and called loudly to Santa Fé. In March she returned bringing another one with her; we named them The Harpies. They both started to call to him; one using the curious "cow-bell" sound sometimes made by crows. Santa Fé did not respond and seemed rather to avoid them, but they continued to come; and in September he came in one day with a bare patch over his eye, obviously having had some sort of a scrap.

A week later awful noises were heard coming from the studio and Dusky was barking furiously outside. Pog found Santa Fé and the bigger of the two crows lying on the floor with claws locked in each other's breasts. She separated them and The Harpy got thrown out. Santa Fé continued to fly with the two birds but they never ventured inside again.

When Santa Fé was about a year old, he began to join us on our daily walk with Dusky; sometimes landing on the dog's back, sometimes on our heads, but never if there was anyone else in sight. We always carried a paper-bag with bits of food to give him, but soon the wild gulls got the idea and wanted a look-in, too, so two paper-bags had to come on the walk. Dusky rather confused matters as he felt it a duty to bark at the gulls so that Santa Fé could feed in peace, and while he was careering about doing this Santa Fé would solemnly pick up the end of his lead and walk along beside us. Perhaps he thought it was we who ought to be on the lead and he was deputising for Dusky.

Like most crows Santa Fé was clever and certainly used his brain, all the time watching everything we did. He had always been intrigued by the sight of Pog brushing and combing her hair, and one day she saw him walking round and round the studio with the comb in his beak looking for the brush. When he could not find it he went to the broom and dustpan and tucked the comb into the floor brush.

He would fly suddenly in at the window while we were having a meal and, like lightning, hurl the tops off tea-pot, sugar basin, salt pot, jam jar, kettle, etc., etc. He picked them up by the knob, and seemed to have a mania that nothing must ever have a lid. He made smash-and-grab raids on all our possessions, hiding them with the utmost care and never forgetting where he had put them.

One Easter Monday while Pog was enjoying a cigarette in the garden, Santa Fé suddenly descended from the sky, in a flash seized a

85

whole packet of twenty out of her pocket, washed it in his bath, then flew to the roof and scattered the contents in every direction. Pog was distraught—it was Bank Holiday and all the shops shut.

He liked best to have his bath in the kitchen sink, and knew quite well the tap must be turned before the water would flow. He would try to turn it with his beak, sometimes with some success, if we did not get there quickly enough.

When in his third year he joined the wild birds again but never forgot us; coming daily for breakfast in the studio and joining us in the fields with Dusky.

One morning instead of going to his pan of food he roused Pog from sleep by walking on her bed, and then deliberately turned his shoulder towards her. To her dismay she saw it was bruised and bleeding. He let her bathe it, and then hopped and fluttered up to the beams. For a week he never attempted to leave the studio. Then after seven more days he took short flights in the room, and the wing seemed healed. On the eighth day we were looking out of the window, wondering if we ought to let him go, when he came and sat between us. The sky was rather stormy and we decided to keep him in a little longer. We were just talking about this when he took hold of the window catch and worked it up and down with his beak. Feeling he knew better than we did we opened the window. He circled round once as in salute and then was off with his usual strong flight.

Santa Fé continued to come and see us, but as each April came round he always failed to appear for three or four days at a time. When he did turn up he was always in a hurry and went off with a mouthful of soft food, evidently for his mate and their young. Apart from this, he seldom missed a day the whole year round. There was certainly a very strong link between him and Dusky, because he never joined us in the fields again after Dusky died. He also came less and less to the studio and Green Hedges and finally never came inside again. We saw him occasionally in the apple tree in the garden, and he would flick his wings at us in recognition when we called, but our intimate contact was broken. He was then in his ninth year.

*　　*　　*　　*　　*

Another bird who had the utmost trust in Dusky was Goidel, a rook brought to us one April as a very forlorn and crumpled-looking baby.

Some Unusual Personalities

We reared him up in Santa Fé's wastepaper basket at Green Hedges, and as soon as he could hop around we took him in the garden with us at our mealtimes. If anything scared him he rushed to Dusky and sat close beside him. When the danger was past he would collect bits of paper, sticks or pennies and push them under Dusky (lying peacefully on the grass) and tuck his fur over the treasures to hide them from sight. He would then sit on Dusky's back or tail and preen his fur.

Goidel took longer flights every day but never went far, until mid-July, when he must have been four months old, and then he stayed away for the night. After that he never again slept in, but returned always at daybreak to my bedroom window, hopping down onto my pillow or bed-rail to enjoy some breakfast; afterwards preening every feather, sometimes for half an hour. He would then join us on and off throughout the day, flying in and out of the window or sitting beside Dusky on the doorstep.

In the autumn I had to go away for ten days, and I wondered very much if when I came back Goidel would have forgotten me.

The first morning after my return I opened my window very early and almost at once he landed on it, but instead of coming straight in as usual, he peered down at me, looking very thin and nervous, and obviously not at all sure. Then his expression changed, he flew down to the window-sill, his head feathers rising with pleasure, and then on to my pillow. He came onto my shoulder as I lay in bed and rubbed his head under my chin in greeting. It really was an absolute expression of affection and pleasure at my return.

No bird has ever shown me quite such individual friendship as this rook while at the same time living an utterly wild life. When he was two years old his visits were less frequent, though he seldom missed his early morning 'date' and was still completely tame and happy with us both, although he would never come inside if strangers were in the room.

In November, when two and a half years old, he ceased to come altogether. We missed him terribly but did not feel too unhappy; he was in perfect condition, absolutely "grown up" and obviously had long ago been welcomed by his own kind (photo, page 152).

We have noticed that rooks when released do not, as a rule, come back to us as jackdaws and as Santa Fé, the crow, did. Goidel is the only one who retained a contact for so long.

The Cry of a Bird

We never found that young birds reared by us and later released have been in any way unacceptable to their own kind. In fact, the contrary is the case. Our free flying birds actually bring their wild friends back with them as if to prove we are "fit to know". This may be because the relationship between us is always one of mutual friendship. We never make pets of the birds, their intelligence demands something more than that. It is a rare privilege to be given their confidence and trust; but it demands a sensitive awareness on the part of the human being to understand even a small part of their individual minds. Each bird, even of the same species, varies in character and mental outlook, some remote and wild, others intimate and fearless—as in the case of Max and Moritz, found deserted in the same nest; and Pepper and Salt, the other baby jacks whose nest came down the chimney. Moritz and Pepper both remained friendly with us for years after release, whereas Max and Salt became wild and aloof soon after they began to feed for themselves, and never became tame.

Birds we have released definitely know the difference between us and strangers, although sometimes the bolder ones will accept our friends. It would be dangerous for the birds' sake to release them before they are aware of this.

*　　*　　*　　*　　*

The only birds we have ever been unable to release because of undue tameness, though fit to fly, are those reared by other people who sometimes bring birds to us not knowing what to do about them.

A bird in this category was Pip, the magpie. We had taken him in as the result of a letter asking us to give a home "to a magpie who had been behaving so badly in the streets of Penzance", that the writer feared for his safety. Our correspondent had adopted Pip as a deserted baby, giving him complete freedom, though he had returned at nights to sleep in the loft. Each morning he would go to a neighbour's yard where he would have his bath in her meat tin, drying off in a nearby blacksmith's shop. This made his feathers more grey than white when brought to us. Unfortunately, Pip had also the habit of helping himself to sausages and fish from open shop windows; he would sit on people's hats and shoes or on the bonnets of their cars. Once he went to sleep, head under wing, in the middle of Market Jew Street, the main street of Penzance, causing a traffic block. Even if Pip had to give up his adventurous life for the sake of his own safety, he so loved human society that we hoped it made up to him for his lack of freedom.

Caw-Caw, the rook, was another bird that had also been reared by hand, and given freedom which she abused to such an extent that her owners feared a price would be put on her head. One day a complaint was made that she had gone into someone's kitchen and torn to bits a pound of special tomatoes. She had taken a £1 note from another house and amused herself by sitting on various clothes lines in the village, and removing the clothes pegs at top speed. She was in fact beyond all control, and everyone was getting angry.

One day her owners returned from Penzance to find no Caw-Caw, and they feared the worst had happened. But a few days later she turned up in Mousehole, five miles from home; and went up to a boy in the village, who fed her, and seeing how tame she was he brought her to us.

We made enquiries and managed to find her worried owners, who asked us if we would keep her until she was reformed. They came over to see her, bringing a special button (stolen by her from a shop) and clothes pegs to comfort her.

She settled in well, accepting us as friends; and after her second year laid eggs annually, taking enormous pleasure in building her nest, until eventually she died suddenly of peritonitis in her fifth year.

We always wished we had known the part played by the people in the early life of a young black-backed gull, still in her first year when sent to us from Southampton, where she had been found lost and starving. Whoever they were, they must have set great store by the bird because she had a golden ring set with amethysts (slightly chain-store) on her leg when she was found. The finders removed the ring for fear it might damage her. She had evidently been reared by hand as she was very tame and desperately hungry and expected to be waited on like a spoilt child, having no ideas as to feeding herself. Some young herring gulls and great black-backed gulls are very slow to mature mentally, but Gertie, as this bird was called when sent to us, surpassed all others. We were asked to help her to become less tame and more suited to wild life before releasing her again.

She grew into a wonderful bird, but at the end of the year was still as tame as ever. The following May she appeared restive, and after walking in and out of the run for a few days she suddenly took off, returning the same week to the roof and then down for some food. This daily routine lasted some time and then she went away and did not come back.

Later that summer we heard of a young black-back at Marazion, just round the bay, who was a great attraction to visitors, being tame enough to feed from their hands. Some people we knew even saved all their scraps during the week, and on Sundays went to Marazion to be met by the gull who would fly either to the roof of their car or down to the beach beside them.

Our suspicions were aroused, especially when at the end of the year the Penzance R.S.P.C.A. inspector was asked to go to Marazion and catch a young black-backed gull who was removing people's hats. Some of these people were intrigued to find a large wild bird so tame and friendly. Others did not appreciate the privilege and the inspector thought the bird would be safer under our control for the present, so brought her to us.

On arrival she seemed completely at home and quite pleased to see us all again and walked about the runs with all Gertie's old poise. There was no doubt as to her identity.

We decided to keep her through that winter of 1959, thinking that by the following spring she should be in her full adult plumage, and that a wild mate would probably break her close contact with humans.

But by then the hospital had passed out of our control and we heard, to our regret, that Gertie had been sent far from home and friends, and released on the other side of Plymouth from a wild bit of coast, over a hundred miles away, when winter was at its worst.

We could only hope she again found humans to befriend her as events had proved she was not yet ready to fend for herself. This we will never know, but there was an interesting sequel:

17 *July*, 1961. The entry in the hospital record on this date is as follows:

"GERTIE RETURNED AFTER SEVENTEEN MONTHS' ABSENCE."

We were called to the hospital on this date to see a great black-backed gull which was standing erect on the ridge of the roof, in full adult plumage, neck proudly upstretched, with all Gertie's old self-assurance. The only two black-backs that had ever fed readily from the hand, after being released, were Drop In and Gertie. This bird was definitely not Drop In (he was always known by his drooping wing), but was she Gertie?

We stood beside her old run, to the top of which she used to return for food after first flying freely; we called her name, she turned towards us, and then came with calm, unhurried flight down to her old feeding place. We offered her food, she looked us directly in the eyes, and then came quietly up and took it with all Gertie's old gentleness from our hands. No snatch and grab, such as Drop In favoured us with.

We have no proof beyond this. But she looked like Gertie, she behaved like Gertie, and in our own minds we were absolutely sure it was her.

Another bird who we imagined had been reared by hand and then escaped, was a jackdaw. She was the exception to all rules, regulations and preconceived ideas. We called her Lazy Daisy because she refused to do anything for herself when first brought to us. As with most of our birds, we knew nothing of her original history; the first we heard of her was that she had flown through an open window in Penzance, and landed on a woman's head as she sat at breakfast. The woman was very taken aback, but shut the window, and rang for help.

When brought to us, Lazy Daisy at once jumped on our shoulders, demanding food. She was utterly fearless, with an abnormal determination to have her own way. Her plumage was poor, and we had to keep her in for about six months.

When released she stayed around all day, returning to sleep at night. She was still quite without fear, and would walk about the sanctuary, untying the shoelaces of unsuspecting visitors. She loved to get inside the coal-bin, making terrible noises; and if anyone ever tried to take a photo of her she would always sit on their camera. This jackdaw surprisingly developed a great interest in rooks, and when Goidel began to fly Lazy Daisy would go with him, heralding his return with a screeching yell, quite unlike any jackdaw call we had ever heard before. In fact, people down in the village used to ask us what kind of bird it was making the strange cry they so often heard coming from the hill. When Goidel eventually left for good Lazy Daisy also disappeared on the same day. However, she returned alone, after two weeks away, as tame and self-opinionated as ever.

After that she spent her time between Green Hedges and the

sanctuary, but never again went away for long at a time. In her fifth year she began to be interested in another jackdaw, a wild one, whom she tried to inveigle into the coal bin. It was all extremely complicated but Lazy Daisy could cope with the most impossible situations. At last, towards the end of March, they decided to build a nest on a deep shelf, high up in the corner of the hospital porch; a commanding but safe position. We gave them a wooden box, and nailed boards round the edge of the shelf. It was a super nest, a small one within a big one, and the porch made a roof over their heads.

They both started building, stealing bits and pieces out of the pigeons' nests from the loft over the porch. The wild bird went farther afield, fetching straw and sticks from all around the place, and Lazy Daisy went back and forth, all day long, getting material from our sitting-room at Green Hedges. Her mind had a constructionist turn, because she concentrated on all the bits of wire she could find. She even carried the toasting fork off in her beak, but it was too heavy and she had to drop it half way to the nest. She made a mighty effort, and dragged the poker from the hearth to the window, but could not engineer it any further. Next she fancied the curly bits of wire in the element of an electric heater. Wood from our firewood box, bits of wool and cotton from the workbasket, and paper torn up into strips were all her contributions to the home. I caught her one day on the desk tearing up letters and finally flying off with an income tax form. By now the nest looked rather like a Council rubbish dump.

When the third week in April came they stayed by the nest all night, and then, on the 25th, an egg appeared. The wild mate sat on it continuously while Lazy Daisy tore about in almost hysterical excitement, still adding material to the nest, and, for very short spells, sitting on the egg while the other bird fed. Now we realized our mistake, and we had to do a little matrimonial adjustment. *He* became Lazy, and following the conventions, his surname became hers, and we named her Daisy. The excitement grew, two eggs arrived, and we began to look forward to the "Daisy Chain".

Then, one day, four weeks after the first egg had appeared, they deserted the nest. When they were not about we looked to see what had happened to the eggs, and found them intact, but when broken open by us there was no sign of life in them. Then to our great surprise we found a pigeon's egg also in Lazy's nest.

On breaking this one open we found a little chick inside, dead, but fully formed. We could only think that Lazy, true to character, was not satisfied with the size of his wife's eggs and had carried one over from the pigeon loft, and deposited it amongst the blue-speckled jackdaw eggs. Once he had been seen in the loft, picking up a pigeon's egg in his beak without breaking it, so, though no one saw the actual transportation from loft to porch, we could think of no other explanation for its being there.

Shortly after this Daisy, the wild bird, did not sleep in any more, and finally departed altogether. Lazy reverted to his bachelor habits, keeping an eye on everyone; including a new batch of young rooks which had been reared by us in the hospital earlier on after having fallen from their nests. They were now released and flying freely, but always returned at night to sleep in trees in the garden. In the morning, when they were fed, Lazy would stand beside them swelling, apparently, with pride, and allow them to eat all the best food without protest. If other birds came down near the young rooks he would chase them off in a rage; he especially disliked crows, but just ignored other jackdaws. Lazy then got a new interest—in money. He would somehow undo my purse if I left it on the table, and proceed to throw the contents about all over the place. Once he flew off with half a crown, which he took to the hospital, but not as a donation. On the contrary; he was seen one day extracting a ten-shilling note from the slit in our money box, and was only just frustrated in time. When we had a new box we had a smaller opening made to outwit him.

He is still flying freely, sometimes sleeping in at night, sometimes roosting outside with his friend the rook, and in January of 1961 he started a new occupation, the censorship of this book. It is most extraordinary how he will fly in at the open window of our sitting-room and land straight on to my manuscript as I sit working at my table by the fire. He is, in fact, at this moment standing on the foolscap. If I am only writing letters he will perch on my chair, and take no notice of what I am doing; but when it is this book I am busy about, the inspection starts. With head lowered as if reading he makes odd jabs at the words. Once when I wanted to add a bit to Chapter VI, already sent for typing, I wrote it on a slip of paper with a note to the typist, and left it ready for the post on the hall table. Some time later I found the envelope ripped open, the slip pulled out, and torn, and a bit missing. Next day I discovered the odd bit in the fruit bowl—on it was written the word "dog". Had I thought Lazy Daisy could read I would not have put it above him to count "dog" as a matter irrelevant to the main subject of the book. He is one of the most outstanding birds ever to come our way (photo, page 111).

*   *   *   *   *

Amongst some of the rooks and crows we have reared up, we have noticed a curious habit. It is the way they enjoy the smoke from a cigarette being puffed into their feathers and under their wings. Pog noticed it for the first time one day when her studio fire was smoking badly. The smoke was being blown back down the chimney and into the room as often happens when the wind is westerly. She had some wire-netting put over the top of the stove (the closed-in type) in case Santa Fé, the crow, should land on the top and burn his feet. This day the smoke was puffing out, in great clouds, worse than usual. Suddenly Santa Fé flew down from the beams and spread himself out on the wire-netting, apparently delighting in the bath of smoke.

We have discovered, by watching our rooks and crows, that it is not at all a universal habit amongst the species, but those birds that do practise it get into a kind of excited ecstasy over it; much as some birds do when spreading themselves out on an ant-heap and allowing the ants to penetrate through their feathers and all over their wings. This is known as "anting". Goidel, the rook, used to like both the ant heaps and cigarette smoke.

One young crow we had used to fly to Pog's shoulder directly she entered the room, spreading his wings and trembling with anticipation as she got her cigarettes and matches. When the height of his excitement was reached saliva would form in his mouth and he would deliberately dribble it down into the inside of the neck of Pog's jersey.

Santa Fé, the crow, used to pick up ants in his beak, very delicately without killing them, and insert them between his feathers on back and wing. He was also an addict to smoke and after enjoying Pog's cigarette he would fly to the chimney on our roof, and have a further and bigger dose of the drug. It caused a kind of sensual satisfaction.

The posture birds take, when revelling in either the ants or the smoke, is much the same as that assumed when having a sun-bath, both wings being outstretched, and the bird flattening itself on the ground, or roof, and the feathers rising with pleasure. When sunning, however, birds seem to be in a semi-swoon and less aware of their surroundings than when stimulated by the ants or the smoke, which create a curious mental excitement.

Chapter XII

OWLS AND OTHERS

THE uncanny call of the owl from the darkness of the night, and its silent, secret flight seem to stand apart in one's mind from the beauty of the daytime birds. But the owls are fascinating in their own mysterious way, with exquisite soft feathers and great round eyes looking so full of wisdom; although their nocturnal habits make them rather difficult to deal with as patients.

One of the first birds brought to us was a Little Owl, found lying on the road at Lamorna, the next cove beyond Mousehole. His legs were completely lifeless, but otherwise he was uninjured. We gave him special tablets from the vet and, in a week, life returned slightly to his legs, and three days later he was able to bend them. He was a wonderful patient, sitting quietly on his hay bed, eating well off egg, raw meat and liver, which we wrapped up in bits of fur or feathers to provide the roughage which all owls must have. Pog arranged a soft heap of cushions on a table in one corner of the room and at frequent intervals he flew from her hands the full length of her studio to this pile, and landed "soft" without ever making a mistake. In this way he was able to get exercise without harm to his legs.

He soon began to grip our fingers, and to stretch his legs a little, but there was no real strength in them, and our hopes that they would recover started to fade. His eyes were bright and alert, and he was so adaptable to life as he now found it that it was difficult to decide not to go on. He, himself, was undaunted and tried to use his legs and to back our efforts to overcome the fate whose shadow was beginning to fall.

After three months the improvement had slowly lessened, and then we knew the time had come. Our veterinary surgeon made the end as gentle and imperceptible as possible, but the sadness of the decision is always there; and none wanted more desperately to live than Mr. Carne, our Little Owl. The post mortem showed incurable neuritis in his legs, which might have been caused by contact with high voltage wires. If this was so the nerves would have been destroyed, and the case hopeless. In later years we had other birds to whom we suspected the same accident had happened; some died at once, or had to be destroyed —a few we saved.

Another springtime a very young tawny owl was brought to us from Penzance. He was starving, and took readily from a paintbrush a baby mash of egg, milk, digestive biscuit and Bemax, mixed with minced raw meat or liver, and little bits of fur or feather. The latter again used as roughage to aid digestion, and so make possible the formation of the pellet which owls to keep healthy must make and expel daily from their mouths. This pellet is a closely woven oval-shaped ball of discarded particles of food, and its contents is particularly interesting to study in a wild bird as it shows what its diet has been.

On the fifth day after arrival, our baby tawny owl made his first pellet; and on the next day we saw him looking at a small dead mouse we had put beside him. He evidently thought he ought to do something about it, but was not quite sure what. Then he solemnly picked it up and stuffed it wholesale into his mouth, using his foot as a hand. The movements of these babies are fumbling and awkward, and very appealing.

We always gave him his last feed as late as possible at night and, as he grew able to fly, we left him free in the room so that he could stretch his wings in the small hours. He soon became wilder, and when about three months old was able to be released, and flew off beautifully.

Another baby tawny owl, which this time unfortunately we were not successful with, was brought to us so young that his eyes were not yet opened, and he was covered with white down. He must have fallen from his nest in some old trees, overhanging the disused quarry. He revived with warmth and enjoyed a slightly heated mash of egg, etc. We called him The Abominable Snowman, because on the second day when he did open his slit of an eye, it had a mongolian look and was red-rimmed. On the third day both eyes opened, but not for long at a time.

He soon began to produce pellets in the usual way, and was eating well, but from the first was very weak on his legs. We got tablets from the vet, and gave him all possible nourishment, but after six weeks he died. The post mortem showed no cause for death.

He was one of the very trusting babies, and we felt sad to have failed him. He loved to sit on our arms and really seemed to enjoy our company. He was also very friendly with a young thrush, who came in about the same time (photo, page 111).

Again at nesting time, two more young tawny owls were found stranded on the road between Penzance and Land's End. How they got there we could not imagine as there were no trees anywhere near and they could not possibly have flown much, being too young. We called them Mayflower and The Pilgrim because *Mayflower II* was actually passing off Land's End on her way to America the day they were found.

They grew apace and as long as we fed them by hand with our usual mixture they advanced at the same rate; but The Pilgrim probably took more than his fair share when they began feeding for themselves and making pellets, as Mayflower did not progress so well then.

One morning, very early, while I was still in bed, I heard angry warning cries from the jackdaws. On looking out I saw a flock of them circling round and round, and diving down towards some elder trees behind the owls' hut. I ran down the path still in my pyjamas, expecting to find a young jackdaw on the ground being attacked by a cat; but there was no sign of anything. I went to see if the owls were all right inside their hut. Mayflower was on the table looking out of a closed window, but there was no sign of The Pilgrim; I then noticed that the wire-netting framework over an open window was wrenched aside, and realised that he must have escaped and be the cause of the row. I got a ladder and climbed up the tree and there he was sitting as cool as a cucumber. He gave me a colossal wink, and though nearly full-grown and perfectly able to fly, did not attempt to do so but let me catch him without any trouble. Directly I had him in my hands the jackdaws dispersed.

The Pilgrim was none the worse for his adventure in the elder tree, and when both owls had been with us about five weeks they began to get wild and seemed ready for freedom. We took them to a wood near to the spot where they had been found, and released them at twilight. The Pilgrim flew strongly, and without hesitation, straight up to the bough of a high tree, but poor little Mayflower flew low into a thicket. We followed her, and found her lying helpless with apparently no power in her legs, and brought her straight home. The vet came and said the legs were fractured, and we could only think she had struck something with great force in her flight into the bushes. The legs were skilfully set and bandaged and for six days she ate well, and made pellets as usual. On the seventh day she would not eat and in twenty-four hours she died. We hardly knew she had gone, death came so quietly.

*   *   *   *   *

We realized that a further stage had been reached in our contact with the wild birds from the way the jackdaws had stopped their warning cries and dispersed the instant I held the young tawny owl safely in my hands, after he had escaped from the hut. It seemed as if they had now accepted us as a "rescue squad" whom they knew and trusted, as opposed to strangers. This was a distinct difference in attitude from the early days when the mother jackdaw had warned her baby against Pog, who was then still looked upon as someone unknown.

We always responded instantly when we heard this warning call. Sometimes we would find a bird on the ground under the high-tension electric pole; sometimes a cat chasing a bird or a baby bird stranded on the ground unable to fly. We have even heard the warning cry given by the wild jackdaws as boys are coming up the hill with a bird in their hands on their way to the hospital, and we have gone down to the road to see what the noise was about. When we have taken the bird from them, and returning with it to the hospital, the jackdaws have stopped calling and flown off.

We had an instance of this yet again when some visitors came to tell us a fledgling herring gull had fallen from its nest on the cliffs over the Mousehole Cave. The parent birds were flying round overhead calling in great distress, and the people were afraid to climb down and rescue the baby for fear they would attack them. This, of course, did not deter Pog, and off she went to see what she could do.

She lowered herself down the rather precipitous cliff in full view of the parent birds, and they continued to wheel round with distracted cries of warning. Then Pog approached the baby slowly, picked it up very gently, and made a cradle for it in her jersey, keeping one hand free for the ascent.

The Cry of a Bird

The visitors stood watching from the top, and then to Pog's horror they started throwing stones at the parent birds, foolishly thinking to protect her. The seagulls naturally were more agitated than ever, but still circled round giving their warning cry. Pog, with much inward wrath, called out to the people to stop, and then, making sure the gulls had seen the baby safely cradled in her arm, began her upward climb. The parent birds then at once stopped calling, but stayed near until Pog reached the cliff top and safety. They then flew high and away, as if they were content to trust the baby to her care.

*　　　*　　　*　　　*　　　*

An alarming-looking bird we were not prepared for was brought to us soon after this—a peregrine falcon. As with all the birds of prey it is the talons rather than the beak that can cause trouble. A friend advised us to use leather gloves, which we did, although this was the first time we had ever done so. Peregrines are the largest of the falcons breeding in Great Britain, the male being fifteen inches long and the female larger (as in most birds of prey). They are distinguished by the slate-grey plumage barred with a darker shade on the upper part. The underside is white with black markings, shading to pale buff on the breast.

Our bird had been found near Newquay with a damaged wing, not actually broken, only rendered useless by a very bad wound, and from his size we judged him to be a male. We got the largest packing-case in Penzance, hastily converted it into a felt-covered house and Excalibur, as we called the falcon, entered into possession. He was a marvellous patient, and never attacked us as we cleared out his house, but sat like an image on his bough, eating large quantities of raw meat and rabbit, and keeping his wounded wing quite still.

In three weeks' time he had completely recovered and we returned him to his own cliffs. When released he rose slowly on the wing and was seen soaring away over the valley to the distant woods.

From these birds of prey it was a sudden change to have to deal with a tiny quail that was brought in only seven inches long, beautiful in its plumage of pale brown with darker stripes, and smooth to the touch as a billiard ball. The quail is a summer resident only, and this one was found in September with an injured wing and damaged eye. He settled in well. We kept him indoors at night, but in an outdoor run all day, and he loved his dust baths. With these, and the sand and grass to help, his plumage stayed in perfect condition. Each evening when we held our hands half open before him on the ground, he would literally dive into them, his smooth, warm body just fitting in when the hands were closed. He would stay quite still like this while we transferred him to his night quarters. We were interested when we were told that at one time in China quails were carried in the sleeves of the mandarins who used them as hand-warmers.

After a year, his wing was strong enough for use in his run, but not, we feared, for migrating, especially as his eye was quite hopeless. Feeling it was lonely for him here, we asked the London Zoo if they would let him join five other quails they had there. They agreed, and the following year he mated with one of them, had triplets, a boy and two girls, which at the age of three months were reported as "looking splendid, as was their father".

*   *   *   *   *

One of the youngest and most interesting birds we ever had was a great tit, found by the roadside, a little bundle of yellow-green fluff, no tail or wing feathers yet grown. He clung to our fingers with his tiny feet, sucking raw egg off a paintbrush as fast as we could give it to him.

In three weeks he had grown up into a perfect bird and was feeding himself, though still cheeping to be fed at nights till quietened with a sup of egg. Tit-bits we called him. When released in the garden he returned to his house for two nights, then joined a crowd of tits, and we thought we had seen the last of him.

In March, nine months later, I was going into the birds' hut to shut them up for the night when something flew across my face and landed on the water butt just in front of me. It was a great tit, deliberately staring at me, his eyes blinking with sleep. I crept slowly into the hut, got some egg, and put it beside him. He devoured it instantly, but made no attempt to fly. By now I was sure it was Tit-bits. He stayed like this for some time looking more and more sleepy but never closing his eyes. It was getting dusk and I felt desperate; as he could not be left like this, I simply had to catch him. Very slowly I put out my hand—he didn't move, so I closed it gently round him and he snuggled down into it. That was what he had wanted all the time. Once on a bough in the hut, he was soon head-under-wing in a deep sleep.

For two days he just ate and slept in his house, then on the third morning he was flying round alert and ready. We opened the door and off he flew, completely restored. This was a most interesting example of definite recognition, shown by flying across my face. He had remembered the place where he was reared and had returned there, evidently tired by a long flight.

Another very beautiful baby that was brought to us was a greenfinch. She had been found helpless in a field at the end of one May, and when she came she was a small green-and-gold ball with all the delicacy of a mimosa blossom—and that is what we called her.

We persuaded her to take food from a paintbrush but she remained weak for three days. Then came a sudden revival, and in ten days she was feeding herself and trying her wings. Soon she was flitting about the garden all the day long, calling "shree, shree, shree" when hungry for food, which she would then take from the tips of our fingers.

For three weeks she returned every evening to the same tree and let us "pick" her off the branch and put her back in her house. But in the first week in July, when she came as usual to the tree, she would not let me catch her. Usually she sat completely still and waited for my hand to close round her, but this evening she flitted about from one branch to another, but did not seem to want to fly away. I was puzzled and finally just held my hand out without movement. She at once came down to it and did a fairy-like dance on the back of my hand, repeating the action several times, while I stood perfectly still, more puzzled than ever, because I was convinced she was trying to tell me something. At last I understood what it was; there on the tree above, watching us, was a most beautiful big greenfinch. The instant I realised it was her boy friend she gaily flew off with him.

She never again slept in, but for four days played in the trees with her friend, feeding from our fingers occasionally; and then one evening she came back into her old tree. She once more did her little dance on my hand; this time the message must have been one of farewell, because we did not see either of them again. We had no fears for her because she would never go to anyone but us, and probably all the greenfinches were seeking new haunts at this time as they also disappeared from the garden.

Two years later a greenfinch built a nest in the bushes which Mimosa had been so fond of. Although she would not feed from our hands, we felt sure it was Mimosa because she had no real fear of us. Then one day there was a terrific "shree, shreeing" from the bird tray at our Green Hedges' window. There was no doubt any more, for there she was with her fat husband and two wonderful Mimosettes. For a week they flew back and forth to the bushes, a golden cloud of fluttering wings.

* * * * *

Just about this time we noticed that we had had ninety-nine different species of birds since we started the Wild Birds' Hospital. We were anxiously waiting to see what the hundredth species would be, and hoping it would be something rare.

At the end of May some children brought us a fully feathered baby bird such as we had never seen before, with soft smoky black plumage and a white patch on the throat. We made an anxious search in the bird book and found he answered to the description of a ring ouzel, a new bird to us, and we acclaimed him as our "100th" with joy.

In the morning we heard familiar squarks, whistles and trills coming from his cage—we knew that voice! Reluctantly we turned up "starling", where we found that the young are completely different in plumage to the adult, and our baby fitted the bill. We called him Little Black Mingo.

He grew apace, flying beautifully in the run; and at the end of June we released him in the fields, saying a rather sad farewell. But the same evening he was back again, peering into the office window where he had been reared. So we caught him and returned him to his usual sleeping quarters.

After this, each morning we let him go; but he would come back and join us for meals in the garden, and at 6.30 each evening would return to the top of the run. When we opened the door for him he would fly straight in through two more runs and go to bed in his usual place.

After two weeks he found a companion whom he deliberately brought to the apple tree to introduce to us—then he stayed away for the nights, coming to the garden by day. In August all the starlings flew off and we saw Little Black Mingo no more until December, when again he came and peered in at the office window. Two weeks later he returned to the top of the run, just to inspect but not wanting to come in. He was now in full speckled plumage, and soon after this he ceased to come any more.

Our hundredth species eventually arrived a month after Mingo first came. It turned out to be nothing more nor less than a lost starving hen with an injured leg.

We had an S O S that a hen had been seen caught by her leg and was struggling in the undergrowth half way down the cliff; so Pog and a friend got strong ropes and, with some farm men to help them, went off to the rescue.

They carefully crept down the cliff till they could reach the hen, finally managing to get hold of her and bringing her up in triumph. One of her legs was strained and swollen.

We found out later where she had come from and that she had been missing a whole month. After this awful adventure we felt we could not let her return to her fate on the farm where she belonged, so the three of us paid 5s. each and became the proud owners of a beautiful, if limping, Rhode Island Red. She was after all the awaited hundredth species—a bit of a comedown from a ring ouzel, but nevertheless she filled a unique position which had to be duly honoured. On the very day we paid the money, Mrs. Hitty Pitty, now her name, laid an egg and continued to do so daily, giving us over sixty that summer.

She fancied herself as matron of the hospital and would strut about all over the place inspecting the "wards", coming at lunchtime to sit on the grass beside us and snatching food from our hands and mouths if she liked the look of it.

Chapter XIII

STRANGERS WITH A PLACE IN OUR THOUGHTS

W E often wish we had kept a record of the people who came to see the birds as well as one of the birds themselves. From every part of the world they have come. All have been interested and some puzzled, like the ones during the war who said, "I suppose you keep birds to provide you with eggs." A few have been critical, but when they have realized that the choice is life or death for the birds, and have seen for themselves the contentment of the ones who cannot fly again, and have heard of those who return for years after release to visit us, these doubters usually end up the most enthusiastic.

Over the years we have had many letters from people asking about our work. The writers generally remain strangers, except in a few rare cases where an unusual friendship is created; the communicating link being the birds.

A brief contact was once made when two African veterinary surgeons from Uganda paid us a visit. They entered with great understanding into the problem of healing completely wild things, and made helpful suggestions. They seemed deeply interested in everything, as were a Hindoo doctor and a doctor from Peru. The last two were especially concerned about the oil contamination problem.

A letter came one day from Wolverhampton from someone completely unknown to us, who had read an account in *The Field* magazine of our sanctuary, and enclosed a gift for the birds. The article had included a photograph of Pog and Phoenix, the rock dove; apparently this had reminded the writer of her own dove, her sole companion in what sounded a very lonely life. She told us she was a secretary shorthand-typist, working for her living in town surroundings, so each Easter we sent her a box of primroses and spring flowers which seemed to give her great pleasure.

Later she wrote that her health was failing and she had had to give her dove to a friend and go into a London hospital. Finally, a very sad letter came; she had been sent back to the Midlands without hope, and had been put in a depressing and uncongenial general ward in a hospital there. We wrote and sent her Easter flowers as usual; no answer came. Then we had a letter from a solicitor saying his client, Miss Mildred Carter, had died shortly after Easter and had left us a legacy of £50 for our birds. So this friend we had never met had given to the Birds' Hospital that money which could have provided her with the comfort of a private room instead of the sad surroundings in which she passed away.

We spent her gift on several desperately needed improvements but reserved some of it to commemorate her loving and unselfish thought in a special way. When later the permanent hospital and sanctuary were built we had a wrought-iron gate made incorporating the design of our symbol of wings in flight. We liked to feel, as we hoped Mildred Carter would too, that it was her gate that opened the way to the sanctuary (photo, page 134).

Another link with a bird lover we never knew came about when a sad-faced Polish lady came and told us in broken English how her brother had died in the war, fighting with Britain. After his death his clothing had been returned to her, and in one pocket she had found some English coins. The brother was a journalist and great bird lover.

His sister had kept the money, 6s. 5½d., until she came to England from Paris which was then her home, determined to give it to some cause which had to do with birds. On passing our gate at Green Hedges she saw "Wild Birds' Hospital". "I knew this was where I had to come," she told us, and went on to say that when she and her brother were young they also had rescued and tried to help wild birds in their Polish home, and his one desire had been to write a book about English birds. Handing us a crumpled paper bag which held the coins, she said, "I have not added to it, as it is from him."

It was a brief visit, we have never seen her again but we touched something very real. We decided to use the money for a telephone pad (though at that time we had no telephone, but were hoping one day to possess one) so that the Polish soldier would, after all, be writing about the birds. It was not easy to get what we wanted at the price. Eventually Strakers of London helped us. I told them the story, sent the actual coins, and they found, for only 6*s*. 11*d*., exactly the right tablet. It now hangs on the wall in constant use, with the old Polish flag painted on it and the inscription "From the Polish soldier who loved birds and freedom".

A family who were strangers, but to whom later we were to feel very near, came over one day while on their holiday, to see the birds. The father, mother, their three boys and little girl were staying in Penzance. We had a very happy time together, the children were interested in everything and we were all sorry to say good-bye.

Soon they returned to their home in Sutton Coldfield. A year later, we had a letter from the headmaster of a school there, saying Neil, the second boy in this family, had lost his life in a road accident. His schoolmates had given so much money for flowers that his mother wanted some of it sent to us for the birds as she knew this was what her son would have liked.

We had always wanted to get an old Trinity House bell to summon us when an injured bird was brought. We suggested this to the parents and they liked the idea extremely.

We consulted our friend, Captain Goodman, Superintendent of the Penzance branch of Trinity House. He told us the old ships' bells were very difficult to get hold of, and he thought in any case a new shining one was better for a child. He offered to choose one specially and found a new ship's bell with a beautiful clear tone. This he had taken on board the *Satellite*, the Penzance Trinity House boat, and the crew shone the bell till it looked like fine gold. The bosun made a bell rope with all the correct knots, finishing up with the "Turk's Head".

We had Neil's name and the date of his birth and death engraved on the bell (he was thirteen years old when he died), also our open wings symbol of release. We never mentioned the amount to be spent to either Captain Goodman or the engraver, but the total cost came just within the sum given. Neil's parents gave the canopy in memory of their son (photo, page 112).

When it was erected in our garden at Green Hedges we wrote and asked the family to stand by for a telephone call from us the next evening. At the appointed hour Pog stood by the bell, and I got through to Sutton Coldfield, telling them to listen. I held the receiver as far out of the window as I could and Pog pealed the bell. The sound went over crystal clear; Neil's bell had made its first call back to his home.

So the bell would sound through the years to come like the child's voice calling for sanctuary for the birds he loved.

Eight years later the parents sent us a gift to mark the day which would have been Neil's 21st birthday. This we spent on a much-needed special bath for the oiled birds. On a small slate tablet we had written "Bird Bath given 19 May 1959 when Neil Jager would have been 21". Neil once more seemed near and was alive in our thoughts.

People were always very kind and generous, and many a time a gift just saved the situation, though for the first twenty-five years we never had a money box. Somehow we had got like the birds in taking no thought for the morrow, and it was extraordinary how things always worked out.

The most remarkable case of this sort was much later on, just before we decided to make over the land on which the sanctuary stood to the R.S.P.C.A. One boundary of the land was a retaining wall of the lane which ran above. It was in a dangerous state and had not been repaired for many years, and we felt somehow we must get it put right before handing over. Jim, our mason friend from the village, told us it would cost between £70 and £100.

We had no means of finding the money except by selling out a small legacy of War Loan. We told Jim to go ahead and let us have the bill as soon as it was finished, when we would realise the War Loan, hoping its value would go up a bit in the meantime.

The bill came in for only £73. We were planning to go to the bank next day to sell the stock, when the afternoon post brought a letter. Inside was a folded cheque and a note from a perfect stranger saying she was sending the enclosed for our birds, to commemorate Coronation Year. I looked at the cheque—it was for £100! Speechless I handed it to Pog, and she collapsed with amazement. She was holding it loosely in her hand when suddenly Santa Fé, the crow, flew in at the window and snatched it from her. This galvanized us to life, and Santa Fé was so surprised at our activity he dropped the wonderful slip of paper.

We took the cheque down and showed it to Jim. Like us he was astonished and overjoyed at the timing of the miracle.

We wrote at once to the kind donor, but felt we had no words to describe properly what an inspired thing she had done.

Nancy Price, the well-known actress, was the means through which our miracle had happened. She has a deep love of birds and had told a friend of our work and it was the latter who had sent the cheque. Our friendship with Nancy Price is one that has existed for years simply in the written word. She first wrote to us, sending a gift for the birds as a token of her rejoicing over the return of her beloved parrot, which had been lost. Later she gave us the wherewithal to build a much-longed-for enclosure big enough for large land birds, and this we called "The Nancy Price Run". Daily her name sounds amongst the birds and reminds us of her encouraging belief in our efforts from the beginning.

CHAPTER XIV

THE VALUE OF LIFE

THE aim of the Hospital and Sanctuary has always been to restore the sick or injured birds to full health and freedom. If this was not possible, we tried to compensate by giving them security, food, and the companionship of their own kind, which, with removal of fear, made life still worthwhile for them. Only when the suffering of a bird was beyond human aid did the decision to destroy have to be made.

From the early days we had kept notes about the ways of the birds brought to us, when they came and what befell them. Pog began with an old book into which she jotted down anything interesting about their individual behaviour. These records were slightly spasmodic, so I continued with a daily diary.

Finally a stranger was up here one day looking at the birds (he later introduced himself as Mark Hindson, a retired Bank Inspector and a great bird lover) and he devised a ring book system for us. This put all the details into an ordered form for reference, and enabled us to keep a faithful account of every bird from Number 1 in 1928 to Number 4066, the last entry for 1959 when Pog and I gave up active work in the Hospital. During these thirty-one years we have had 116 species under our care.

We never considered ringing birds cured and released by ourselves—doing so would have been of no benefit to them, only of interest to us. This attitude has been strengthened by hearing of authenticated cases of small birds being harmed and handicapped by the extensive ringing practised today.

When the numbers increased we thought we would have a collective name for those birds which only stayed a very short time before recovering and flying off; these we called "Tourists". Those that died very soon, or had to be destroyed at once because they were past all help, we found it difficult to find the right name for. We decided to call them "Pippa's Shadows", after Browning's

The Value of Life

Pippa Passes, the story of the young girl who sang as she passed by, so bringing comfort to the sad, the sick and the suffering, unknown and unseen.

As the story of each bird is completed we end the page with a sign:

⌒⌒   spread wings for a release

——   a black line for death

══   two black lines for a destruction which is to us a double death

We are acutely aware of the irrevocable nature of destruction and only make the decision when, for the bird's sake, there is no question of any other. Life is of value to the bird as to ourselves.

We have always felt too from the beginning that death should come to them unaware. To confine a wild thing in a lethal box seemed a terrible way to end its life. The humane killer was instantaneous, but again the bird went out in fear, this time through being forcibly held in position for the shot.

Then, at last, the right way was found. An injection was given by trained hands, then the bird was put on a bed of hay in a quiet place, where death came gently as it slept.

*   *   *   *   *

On looking back over the years we realise how much we owe to the unfailing kindness and attention of our local veterinary surgeons. They came at whatever hour we needed the help of their skill and knowledge, giving as much care to a wild bird as they would to a valuable pedigree bull. We carried out the treatments advised, gave the prescribed medicines and followed instructions generally. This, with what the birds taught us themselves, was the basis of the curative side of our work.

We soon discovered that the fundamental rules of warmth and quiet were the greatest help in allaying shock and the natural fear of a wild bird held in human hands probably for the first time. Rooks, especially, we have found to be more nervous than crows and jackdaws, though belonging to the same family; they are not afraid of us once their confidence is gained, but are more easily startled and very highly strung, thus necessitating special care during treatment.

We always tried to let all birds get used to their surroundings, giving them conditions as natural as possible, before attempting to treat them. Many birds that were brought were suffering, not so much from injuries, as from exhaustion caused by hunger, cold, and flying long distances; or, of course, from illness which was beginning to get the upper hand.

The best restoratives are often just water, a little concentrated food (halibut oil, egg and vitamin powder) and a deep sleep. A field-fare, for instance, that came in the hard frost of 1956 was starving and weak, but would not look at food until he had drunk great quantities of water. Then he slept and in a week was completely recovered and flew off again. We called him The Dipsomaniac.

Tit-bits, the great tit, who came to us tired out, was restored as much by sleep as he was by food and water; and so was our Viking, the gannet, who went into a very deep sleep soon after he came. On the other hand, "head under wing" accompanied by a drowsiness instead of peaceful sleep, is often a prelude to death in small birds.

As we live by the sea, a great number of the birds brought to us were covered with the black waste oil discharged by ships. We never attempted to clean oiled birds until their first exhaustion was overcome and they had taken a little nourishment. Gentle warmth, and overhead protection given by turning a large box on its side, with a bed of soft material, seemed to give them a sense of security so essential to their chance of recovery. This chance also depended very much on the degree of oil contamination and the length of time which had elapsed before they had been brought to us, for speed in getting attention to the bird is of utmost importance.

The oil can be removed if care and common sense are used; but the, so far, unsolved problem is how to overcome the internal damage caused by the swallowing of the oil, and by its absorption through the skin. Only mild solvents should be used for cleaning the feathers, paraffin and petrol being fatal to the bird. For those birds that were not too badly contaminated the veterinary surgeon used to prescribe a mineral oil, which we found gave good results. Applied a little at a time, it loosened the black oil which could then be removed with cotton wool. If the birds are not in too bad a state, Fuller's Earth can be sprinkled into the feathers as an absorbent. But for really bad cases something quicker in action must be used.

Although we have tried many preparations with success, some

recommended by others and some tried out first by ourselves, we do not feel justified in mentioning them by name for fear of causing inadvertent harm, which can so easily happen through inexperienced use. No-one, as far as I know, has found the perfect solvent which at the same time does no damage. If they had, I am sure they would be only too happy, as we should also be, to make it known.

Whatever means is chosen to clean oiled birds it must not be overdone, and the final stages should be followed (with most solvents) by a quick rinse in slightly soapy water. We have used, as a rule, small quantities of Lux flakes, or Liquid Lux for the purpose, and rain water, if procurable. The cleansing should not be attempted in a single operation, but repeated each day as necessary.

After the complete removal of the contaminating oil from the feathers, the birds must be kept dry until strong and fit. Then they have to be got used to water again. We would first give a daily sprinkle from a watering can, and next would let them splash in a large shallow pan of water, but not allow them to get really wet. Finally they would go into a rock-and-cement bath, shallow at one end and deep enough at the other for them to swim in.

We found, from sad experience, that letting an oiled bird get immersed in water, and thoroughly wet, before the right moment had come, would undo any progress previously made and it would not recover.

In the early days we used to take the small diving birds, which we had cleaned from oil, down to the rocks to swim in deep pools before their final release; or else we would fetch sea-water up from the shore for them. But later, when it was a physical impossibility to do this, we did not find any deterioration in the birds' condition as a result of having fresh water.

Oiled birds must never be released after cleaning till absolutely strong and upright on their feet; the air sacs must inflate and bodies be firm yet buoyant when held in the hand with wings free. If the beat of the wings is not strong and swift, the bird is not ready to go. Nor is it ready if the feathers remain waterlogged after swimming in a bath.

Restoring these birds to freedom cannot be hurried; great patience and observation are needed at every stage. Given right conditions and understanding, they are content in captivity, usually eating with great appetite pieces of herring, pilchard or filleted whiting cut into narrow strips about two inches long and given in a bowl of water. Halibut oil should be given on arrival, a drop on a piece of fish, and continued daily till first exhaustion is overcome.

For lack of balance in any bird we have found raw egg given often, and in small quantities, is a wonderful help. A jackdaw once came, for example, which was quite unable to balance. It pitched forward, flung its head backwards and seemed semi-conscious. We feared it would have to be destroyed, but the vet came and told us to try the egg first. It worked and, after a week of this diet, the bird was completely normal and was eventually released in perfect condition.

Another time a magpie was brought to us which had been caught by the beak in a trap. It was almost unconscious and both its eyes were closed, with matter oozing from them; and only the whites showing when the eyelids were lifted. Its brain was too clouded to enable it to eat for itself, but it swallowed hungrily whatever food we put right into its mouth.

We bathed its eyes and fed it often on raw egg and other nourishing food, and it was quite passive all the time. On the fifth day there was a great change, both eyes were normal, bright and clear. It became absolutely wild and able to feed for itself, and two days later we released it, a perfect bird.

A large number of birds arrived at the hospital with broken wings and we tried various ways of mending them, but finally found Elastoplast was the best. It held the break in position, and the birds could not peck it off, as they had tried to do with bandages, etc. If the fractures were very bad we always asked the vet to come and deal with them.

We seldom attempted to tie up the broken wings of small birds, such as sparrows or chaffinches, but kept them in a fairly small house with soft stuff on the floor, and with a very low bough to perch on. The wing did not always set true, but many times it knitted together quite strongly, and the bird was able to fly well in the end; also in this way the wing did not get stiff through inaction while healing.

We had post-mortems whenever possible. Quite often no definite cause for death could be found, but the following list taken from our records shows the types of trouble that some of the examinations revealed.

The Value of Life

Sea Birds	Oiled Birds	Land Birds
Internal haemorrhage	Ruptured liver capsule	Thorn-headed worm
Peritonitis	Obstruction in bowel	Peritonitis (parasitic)
Fungoid disease	Inflammation of bowel	Inflammation of bowel
Liver disease	(parasitic)	Diphtheric condition of
Parasites	Liver disease	throat
Pneumonia	Gizzard trouble	Fatty degeneration of
Avian T.B.	Worms	liver
Jaundice	Fungoid infection of the	Enteritis
Haemorrhage of the brain	air sacs	Avian T.B.
Paralysis	Enteritis	Anaemia
Enteritis	Oil in lungs	Toxaemia from joint in-
Kidney trouble	Fatty degeneration of liver	fection
Heart trouble and anaemia	Haemorrhage from bowel	Paralysis due to injury
Inflammation of bowels	(deficiency of vitamins)	on left side of brain
Tumour on brain	Peritonitis and pleurisy	Gape worm
Small puncture left lung and lung filled with maggots		
Nerve injury		

*   *   *   *   *

Many things had to be considered when releasing a bird. First, of course, the bird's absolute fitness. Then the month of the year, the weather, the state of the tide with the seabirds, and even the time of day; all had to be taken into account.

Storm petrels and Manx shearwaters we took down to the rocks at dusk; they refused to take off in daylight. Swifts and swallows had to be launched in the air as they cannot get away well from the ground. Gannets and shearwaters we took to the highest part of the rocks to give as much air lift as possible under their great wings.

To release herring gulls we simply opened the door of the run, let them walk out of their own accord, up the steps, and on to a high wall. Usually they took their bearings from there, focused their eyes on the distance (instead of on nearby objects as they do in captivity) and flew off calmly and well (photo, page 42).

An interesting individual release was that of a starling. This bird was probably an old patient returned, because he seemed definitely to recognise Pog as she worked inside the run. She noticed that he was going round in circles outside on the wire-netting immediately over her head, and moving with her as she moved. She called to me, and eventually we lured him to the ground with food and caught him.

He was very tired and hungry but recovered in a few days. We opened the door of the "little birds" house and he flew out strongly. Once outside he rose in an absolutely perpendicular way to a considerable height, and then, suddenly, turned off at a right angle in a straight line to the north. It was as if he were picking up some definite current of air on which to resume his travels.

Mallards we always released on water protected from shooting. Three of them we let go on a lake a few miles away. We chose a muddy bank with a slope about two yards wide going directly down to the water, and with a thicket of reeds and tall grasses on either side. The three birds stood quacking and surveying the scene. Then the duck, ignoring this easy access to the lake immediately in front of her, proceeded to tunnel her own way through the thicket into the water. The two drakes followed her through the tunnel, all three distrusting our choice of a clear way.

Thrushes and blackbirds we took for release to a nearby copse where there is a small stream, but quite often within a few days they returned to our garden. Birds which were adult when brought to us we freed as near as possible to the places where they were found, but baby birds, when fully grown, we released here as this was the place they knew best.

Jackdaws, which were adult birds when brought to us injured, may return for food, after release, but never to sleep inside. On the other hand, those brought in as babies and reared up here, very often do return inside to sleep for some time. This is the "home" they remember, and as good fosterparents we welcome them back through the little window made specially for them in the run, which is not closed finally till nightfall and is opened or them again in the morning.

As I have stated before, some young birds go wild at once on release, others return only for food. Generally speaking it is the more weakly, and slow to develop, birds that return inside to sleep. Perhaps instinctively they understand their need for sanctuary, and have the intelligence to know where it can be found. Or maybe there is always a wise jackdaw amongst them, like our Nigger of the early years, who will not allow them to face the world until they are ready to deal with it.

*   *   *   *   *

While we have been trying to help and restore the birds, our gradually increasing awareness of their way of life has met with a response from them, and a happy acceptance of each other been brought about.

We have found that it is not necessarily those birds that we have known the longest with which we have had the greatest intimacy.

The Value of Life

Although Pog and I have followed the lives of the two herring gulls, Rider and Hedger (photo page 54), so closely for the last eighteen years, we never feel we have made the personal contact with them that we have so often made with jackdaws, rooks, crows and smaller birds.

Seabirds seem more detached from mankind; perhaps because their horizons are more distant and their bond greater with the sea and the air than the land birds, who share nature more fully with humans, in their mutual need of the gifts of the earth. However that may be, the link with seabirds seems harder to make.

With the small diving birds, the guillemots, the razorbills and puffins, the contact is different. Once the birds' confidence is gained it is rather as if they had put their faith in a providence which could not desert them. They are highly sensitive and nervous birds, and fear can easily replace trust. We have always tried our hardest not to fail them in this way. A betrayal of this trust is rather like the betrayal of a young child who has put its faith in a grown-up.

Pog had completely won this trust when she once had to have ten guillemots and razorbills living in the studio with her for lack of room elsewhere. She fenced off a big corner, and at feeding times would take down the barrier. At once they would come flocking out towards her with fluttering wings, like a host of little angels.

When they had fed to repletion, she would hold out her arms and guide them gently back, saying: "Now all God's children go to bed"; and back they fluttered, happy and content (photo page 53).

These diving birds always seem to accept us as part of life, quite impersonally, not questioning who we are, or where we come from. But with the land birds there is definitely a more personal contact. In many cases they do, without doubt, recognize us individually, and seem "pleased to meet" even after their return to wild life.

Some of them not only greet us out of doors in the garden or fields, but come right into the studio and to all the rooms at Green Hedges, and are completely unafraid. They fly up to the beams or on to the table, on to the backs of our chairs, inspecting the desk and drinking and eating from special dishes of food they know will be ready for them. We have had Panorama, the thrush; Tippecanoe, the blackbird; Atticus, the robin; and Lazy Daisy and Pepper, the jackdaws, all in the room at the same time with no antagonism shown between them.

Friendship between us and the birds is intangible but very real, though the degree of intimacy does vary with each bird. To try to follow the working of a wild bird's mind is intensely interesting, but can only be done by living with them, and on their terms. This we have always tried to do, and have been rewarded by so finding a meeting-place with nature in the wild.

After thirty years it seems to us that the link can be made. The mind of the human becoming aware of, and responsive to, the mind of the bird, whose confidence and trust is thus won. It may be at that instant we go back to the awakening of all consciousness, making an intangible bridge of communication with every living thing.

Perhaps that is why each decision to cut that invisible reality hurts so badly. We have lived very close to life and death here with our injured birds, and we feel deeply the contrast between the living bird held in our hands, breathing the air we breathe, seeing what we see, struggling, as we humans struggle, to survive—and then—the end, the stillness and the silence.

CHAPTER XV

WHAT OF THE FUTURE?

WITH the passing of the years we began to realize that we would have to revise the birds' philosophy of "taking no thought for the morrow" with some plan for the future which would still hold to the spirit of the past. We had no money with which to endow the Sanctuary, but could not break faith with the birds or the children by closing down.

Through many winter evenings we talked over the problem. Had we failed at the impossible or was there a way out?

Then our minds were made up for us by the boy who had brought us Brighteyes, now a man over thirty, and others like him who had known the Hospital all their lives. When we were talking to the former about our difficulties one day, he said, "But I never remember the time when there wasn't a birds' hospital here."

Then a young fisherman came to us one terrible night of wind and rain with an exhausted, starving seagull. As he handed it over he said, "Miss Gleeshus, whatever should we do without you both?" That settled it—we had to find a way.

We decided to write to the R.S.P.C.A., who, ever since Colonel Stordy's visit in 1939, had faithfully sent us their weekly grant, and had also borne the cost of many improvements and repairs. As a result of our letter in 1951 the chief secretary came down to talk things over.

We told him it would take much money to run and maintain the Sanctuary, as it now was. The employment of staff, the building of a reception house with new enclosures and houses for the birds, would be costly, and every year the numbers of patients would increase.

He replied, "We are aware of this and are prepared to do it." We told him we would give the Society the land on which the Hospital had started and grown, if in return they would take it over and continue to run it on our lines, but on a permanent and lasting basis. To this he also agreed.

We felt the way had been found. There was hope now that, in the years ahead, the wild birds would still be loved and cared for in this Sanctuary which had become their own.

But much work still lay ahead for Pog and me, before this hope could become a reality. We had to direct all our thoughts and energies towards making plans for the new buildings so badly needed to house all the different kinds of birds.

The main building was to have as many bird houses in it as possible. There were to be outdoor runs leading from it, and a pigeon loft made in the roof. The front door was to open into a small room for use as an office, and to receive visitors. Later, when it was built, we found the word "office" too grand a name to live up to; and, in fact, because of its warmth and comfort from the day-and-night stove we soon gave it over to the more weakly birds.

Then we had to plan a new concrete house for jackdaws, rooks, etc., to replace Pog's old hut which now was in a state of dissolution; all this we had to fit in with our daily work.

We made a Deed of Gift of the land to the R.S.P.C.A., which was duly signed in August 1953, and they appointed an architect to make proper plans from our ideas. The land, being on such a steep slope, presented many difficulties as far as building was concerned, but he dealt very successfully with all these.

At last, building permits were obtained from the authorities and all the practical difficulties overcome. Then, in Coronation year, our castle in the air began to materialise. The builder brought great blocks of time-worn granite for the base of the new hospital and these began to rise in a wonderful wall which fitted in with the surroundings. He told us the granite had come from the old workhouse at Madron, recently demolished, and we liked the thought of these stones having come to rest with us— stones which in their time must have witnessed much sadness as well as giving shelter to the homeless.

One day, when this wall was about four feet high, the two men building it came to us and said, "We would like for you to lay a stone. There won't be any bands or bunting, but we have chosen a stone you will remember." This completely unexpected thought gave us great pleasure.

Never was there a more homely laying of a foundation. We

went with the men and found some beautifully mixed cement and shining trowels, and a stone different from all the others. This we laid carefully and said: "May God bless this house and all that therein shall dwell."

The following year the main building was completed and we moved in. A new board was put up at the entrance calling it for the first time "The R.S.P.C.A. Wild Birds' Hospital"; although it was not until two years later that we handed over all financial responsibility.

Feathers, a five-year-old rook, was the first permanent resident in the new building. We had been very worried at the thought of moving her from her old quarters in Pog's hut, because she was an extremely old-fashioned, not to say Victorian, character, who got the "vapours" if everything was not just so. Pog had made an intensive study of her, and tried always to anticipate her needs. She had made a big outdoor run for Feathers, but the latter refused to use it, preferring a ramshackle and much smaller one. She had a nice-sized indoor house with one corner for nest building, and expected Pog to provide dozens of sticks, and to tear up a whole *Times* newspaper every day, which she in turn could rip up into smaller pieces, more convenient for use. Soon she had completely filled her house with torn-up paper and sticks, so that it was all nest and no house.

She laid eggs every year and did not seem to mind the absence of a mate; instead of children of her own she adopted all the wild jackdaws outside, who would almost queue up for the bits of food she would push through the wire-netting to them.

When all was ready in the new building we carried her to her fresh home. To our amazement she approved the arrangements, and almost at once began to build a nest. Later we gave her a companion but she didn't think he was much class and kept him firmly in his place. She never mated, preferring her prim and proper existence, and enjoying an occasional cigarette with Pog.

She had been with us twelve years, when she began to fail, and, although she still flicked her wings at us in greeting each morning, it was not long before she died, peacefully, in her sleep.

We had a record number of birds brought to us during the year (489 in addition to those already here), and it was due to the new hot-water system, electricity and proper heating facilities that we were able to cope with them all. At this time we were still doing all the work ourselves. The final hand-over could not come until all the building was finished, and until we had trained someone to look after the birds and to carry on after we gave up. This was to be the most difficult problem of all. Advertisements brought many applications but it was hard to find the right person.

As a result of this, one evening a telephone call came from London bringing a suggestion from Mr. Max Robertson of the B.B.C. which we longed to refuse, but finally accepted, succumbing to his persuasive voice. He told us he had seen our advertisement for staff and that he was doing a series on T.V. for the programme called *Panorama* which was based on unusual notices in the Personal Columns of the Press. So far they had interviewed the advertisers in the B.B.C. studio, but now he wanted to bring the camera to the job, and had chosen our advertisement as one likely to be suitable. He lured us on by saying never would we have a wider field for our needs to be made known.

The day was fixed, the sun was shining, and we rose at crack of dawn to get our work done before the invaders arrived. At nine o'clock the procession appeared. Mr. Robertson, the producer, the photographer, the assistants, the camera and the tape recorders. We were completely outnumbered! The occupation lasted all day, but under such kindly direction that the birds did not mind, and we survived.

Neverest, the jackdaw, took the liveliest interest in all the proceedings, flying around the whole time, posing for the camera, and chattering his comments from the roof.

A baby thrush came in at this time so we called her "Panorama"; she appeared on T.V. as the youngest inhabitant, sitting on Pog's hand and captivating the photographers with her confidence. This trust she has never lost. For six years she has been with us and is still here, flying freely in the garden, and in at our Green Hedges window to join us indoors. If we are having meals on the lawn, she is there, too, holding us up at frequent intervals for snips of cheese which we carry about in tins in our pockets for her benefit. `

Mr. Robertson was pleased with his day, but we looked forward with some trepidation to seeing ourselves as others would see us. It was to be a double shock, as this was also the first time we had ever looked at a television programme.

In consequence of all this we had scores of visitors during that summer, and we were amused at the comments they made as they came up the steps. "Oh, there she is" or "That's the one". We were being matched up with *Panorama*.

It also brought us many applications for the job. The first was a wire the following day demanding: "Keep the job for me, arriving Sunday" and signed with a man's name. We telegraphed back, saying: "Await letter." But it was of no avail. A strange barrow-boy type, with wild eyes, turned up. We felt he was an escapist from something unhappy. We pointed out the advertisement had been for a girl, and therefore we could not offer him the job. He took it well, but never looked at the birds or showed any interest in anything; just departed as suddenly as he had come.

A letter then came from a woman who besought us to have her; she was "losing her soul by selling nylon stockings". Another came from a girl who wrote that she thought the job would suit her as she liked an open-air life and enjoyed boating, swimming and riding.

We had endless letters from children, asking questions and wanting to work here. One was an almost "baby letter" from a little girl of about five or six, saying she would come and help us. This was followed next day by one from the mother, who explained the letter had been written and posted completely without her knowledge and she hoped we did not mind. We learnt a lot about human nature by all this but it did not end our search.

We eventually found somebody we thought might be suitable. But now that more staff had to be employed, we were faced with the difficulty of finding accommodation for them. Lodgings and furnished cottages did not seem to work. Then, by another of our miracles, we heard by pure chance that the owners of the house below us on the hill, were going to Australia. We asked them to give us four days' refusal; and rang up the R.S.P.C.A. headquarters, pointing out what a wonderful chance it was to provide living quarters for the girls if only someone could come down and see it. The assistant secretary came and agreed it was the answer. The Society generously and wisely took the opportunity and secured the house.

The obtaining of furniture was the next concern. The personal kindness and understanding of Mrs. Lee, a member of the R.S.P.C.A. Council, made it possible for us to spend up to £150 on doing the job. At first this seemed a fortune, but after spending £50 on beds and bedding, we had to resort to auctions for tables, chairs and cupboards. Pots of paint helped to enhance everything and the final result was simple but adequate, and we only spent four pennies over the £150!

*   *   *   *   *

So our work for the birds in the hospital finished at the end of 1959—and new hands took over. But not many months went by before we were made to realize that it was not the end between us and the birds.

By some means of communication unknown to us, the older ones seem to have conveyed to the newcomers (birds we have neither known nor healed) that we are still here if they need us, at the studio and at Green Hedges. When released back to wild life they come to our windows and into our rooms. The new ones come at first shyly, then with confidence and trust, finally recognizing us with a flick of the wings, such as our old bird friends give us in greeting.

Here is our real reward. The birds themselves are conferring on us the lasting honour of calling us their own. Once more Nigger's thread of gold is woven into the pattern of our lives.

Now, what of the future, when we are no more? Will the Sanctuary still hear the ring of Neil's bell? The sound of many wings, soaring to freedom, resting in contentment or folded in the final peace? Will the loving hearts and willing hands be there to hold the course we have tried to set?

If this be so, we can close our chapter with gratitude in our hearts to those who come after, and with everlasting memories of all those birds we have known and loved.

APPENDIX I

The 116 species treated at the hospital between 1928 and the end of 1959 (4,066 birds in all).

Auk, Little
Bittern
Blackbird
Blackcap
Budgerigar
Bullfinch
Buzzard
Canary
Chaffinch
Chiffchaff
Coot
Cormorant
Corncrake
Crossbill
Crow, Carrion
Cuckoo
Curlew
Diver, Great Northern
— Red-throated
Dove, Rock
— Turtle
Duck, Eider
Dunlin
Falcon, Peregrine
Fieldfare
Flycatcher
Gannet
Godwit, Black-tailed
Goldcrest
Goldfinch
Greenfinch
Guillemot
Gull, Black-headed
— Common
— Great Black-backed
— Herring
— Lesser Black-backed
Hawfinch
Hen, Rhode Island Red
Heron

Hoopoe
Jackdaw
Kestrel
Kingfisher
Kittiwake
Knot
Lapwing
Linnet
Magpie
Mallard
Martin, House
Moorhen
Nightingale
Nightjar
Owl, Barn
— Little
— Tawny
Oyster-catcher
Petrel, Fulmar
— Leach's
— Storm
Phalarope, Grey
Pigeon, Racing
— Wood
Pipit, Meadow
— Rock
— Tree
Plover, Golden
— Ringed
Puffin
Quail
Raven
Razorbill
Redwing
Redstart, Black
Robin
Rook
Sanderling
Sandpiper, Common
— Purple

Scoter
Shag
Shearwater, Great
— Manx
Shelduck
Skua, Great
Skylark
Snipe
Sparrow-hawk
Sparrow, Hedge
— House
Starling, Common
— Rose-coloured
Stint, Little
Swallow
Swan
Swift
Tern, Arctic

Tern, Common
Thrush, Mistle
— Song
Tit, Blue
— Great
Turnstone
Twite
Wagtail, Grey
— Pied
Water-rail
Wheatear
Whimbrel
Whinchat
Whitethroat, Lesser
Woodcock
Woodpecker, Green
Wren, Common
Yellow Hammer

APPENDIX II

SUMMARY FROM 1928 UNTIL 1951 OF THE NUMBERS OF BIRDS AND THEIR SPECIES

Auk, Little	4	Pigeon	69
Blackbird	29	Pipit, Meadow	13
Budgerigar	1	— Rock	1
Canary	1	Plover, Golden	1
Canis (not a bird!)	1	—Ringed	1
Chaffinch	22	Puffin	7
Coot	1	Quail	1
Cormorant	1	Razorbill	49
Corncrake	2	Redwing	57
Cuckoo	1	Redstart, Black	1
Curlew	2	Robin	21
Diver, Great Northern	3	Rook	20
— Red-throated	1	Sanderling	1
Falcon	1	Sandpiper	1
Fieldfare	1	Shag	16
Gannet	4	Shearwater, Manx	1
Godwit, Black-tailed	1	Skua	1
Goldfinch	6	Skylark	1
Greenfinch	13	Snipe	1
Guillemot	191	Sparrow, Hedge	5
Gull, Black-headed	11	— House	19
— Common	5	Starling, Common	67
— Great Black-backed	67	— Rose-coloured	1
— Herring	365	Stint, Little	1
— Lesser Black-backed	4	Swallow	7
Heron	1	Swift	17
Jackdaw	219	Tern, Arctic	1
Kittiwake	12	— Common	1
Lapwing	6	Thrush	49
Linnet	3	Tit, Blue	5
Magpie	4	— Great	1
Mallard	1	Turnstone	11
Martin	3	Twite	17
Moorhen	2	Wagtail, Grey	2
Nightingale	1	— Pied	2
Owl, Barn	1	Whinchat	2
— Little	3	Woodcock	2
— Tawny	1	Woodpecker, Green	1
Oyster-Catcher	5	Wren	4
Petrel, Fulmar	1	Yellow Hammer	14
— Storm	4		

Total number of birds treated in this period—1,497

Appendix II

81 Different Species
{
Herring Gulls   24%
Jackdaws   14%
Guillemots   12¾%
Rest   49¼%
}

100%

(i.e. half of the birds belong to
the first three species).

Died or Destroyed   978
Released   408=27.2% of total—a
gradually increasing
percentage.

Patients in Hospital   111

1,497

In looking at these figures it must be remembered that wild birds
only allow themselves to be caught when their condition is pretty
desperate; therefore the number of complete cures is bound to be
relatively small and the number of deaths great. Our average of
releases over the years kept pretty even, usually between 25% and 34%.